SOMETHING WAS MISSING

SOMETHING WAS MISSING
*Until God, Though Faith, Gave Joy and Peace
And The Full Assurance of Salvation*

By
John Stormer

LIBERTY BELL PRESS
Post Office Box 32   Florissant, Missouri

ALSO BY JOHN STORMER

None Dare Call It Treason
The Anatomy of a Smear
The Death of a Nation
Growing Up God's Way
None Dare Call It Treason — 25 YEARS LATER
None Dare Call It Education
Betrayed By The Bench

SOMETHING WAS MISSING
By John Stormer
ISBN 978-0-914053-18-3

PRINTED IN THE UNITED STATES OF AMERICA
Copyright 2010

All rights reserved. No part of this book may be reproduced or transmitted in any form or by any means electronic or mechanical, including photocopying, recording, or by any information storage or retrieval system without permission in writing from the Publisher, except for brief quotations in reviews or critical articles and essays.

Library of Congress Cataloging-in-Publication Data:

1. Catholicism 2. The Bible 3. Salvation 4. Baptism
5. The Mass 6. Communion 7. The Papal System

LIBERTY BELL PRESS
Post Office Box 32
Florissant, Missouri 62032

CONTENTS

Introduction - Many People Leave The Faith In Which They Grew Up vii
Chapter 1 - A Good Catholic Upbringing — But Something Was Missing 1
Chapter 2 - A Full Time Job At Age 15 Brings Spiritual Challenges 7
Chapter 3 - Moving To A New Job Brought Something More Important 11
Chapter 4 - Fear About An Airplane Trip Helped Me Find What Was Missing 23
Chapter 5 - Learning What Was Missing Brought New Responsibilities 31
Chapter 6 - Question: John, Why Did You Leave The One True Church? 39
Chapter 7 - Has Christ's Early Church Been Changed In Any Way? 45
Chapter 8 - Should Church Traditions Conflict With The Bible? 59
Chapter 9 - Baptism In the Bible: Why, Who, When and Where? 65
Chapter 10 - Why Do Few Churches Preach "Ye Must Be Born Again?" 71
Chapter 11 - The Catholic Mass 75
Chapter 12 - Can Christ Be Re-Sacrificed Daily On Catholic Altars 77
Chapter 13 - Does Taking Communion Feed The Soul? 83
Chapter 14 - The Papal System 91
Chapter 15 - Some People Are Saved — But Many Are Not 101
Chapter 16 - The Church You Attend Will Greatly Shape Your Life 109
ORDER FORM 115, 117

ABOUT THE AUTHOR

As a best selling author of six books, John Stormer has encouraged many to fulfill their responsibilities to the Lord, their families and America.

From 1977 until 2008, Stormer taught two Bible studies for elected officials in the Missouri Capitol each week during the legislative sessions.

A native of Altoona, Pennsylvania, he attended the Pennsylvania State University and graduated from California San Jose State University after Korean War service as an Air Force historian and editor. For years, he was listed in Who's Who In America and is a member of the American Legion and Rotary International. He has honorary degrees from Manahath School of Theology (1965) and Shelton College (1976).

He and his wife, Elizabeth, are 55 year residents of Florissant, Missouri, a St. Louis suburb. Their daughter, Holly, and her husband Steve Hartzell, are the parents of the Stormer's four grandchildren.

Introduction

MANY PEOPLE LEAVE THE FAITH IN WHICH THEY GREW UP

But as it is written, Eye hath not seen, nor ear heard, neither have entered into the heart of man, the things which God hath prepared for them that love him. But God hath revealed them unto us by his Spirit.
—I Corinthians 2:9-10a

NEARLY ONE THIRD OF U.S. ADULTS have left the faith and the churches in which they were brought up. That estimate comes from a widespread survey of 35,000 adults done in 2007. The study was conducted by the prestigious Pew Forum on Religion & Public Life.

Both Catholics and Protestants are leaving the churches of their childhood. They either choose another faith or no religion at all, the Pew survey showed.

Commenting on the survey, *Catholic World News*, said:

If they qualified as a separate denomination, the Americans who have deserted the Catholic Church of their childhood would constitute the third largest religious group in the country, with 10.1% of the total U.S. population.

The Catholic Church lost more members than any other group. However, the total number of Catholics remained relatively stable because of Catholic immigrants.

No reasons were given in the press reports on the survey for why people change churches. A study on why Catholics and multitudes of Methodists, Baptists and others have left the churches in which they grew up might show that they came to see or sense that *Something Was Missing* in their churches and their lives. That is the title of this book.

Because *Something Was Missing*, people who were taught the foundational essentials of the Christian faith often never come to a personal relationship with Jesus Christ. A real personal relationship with Christ produces joy and peace and the total assurance of salvation.

As the author of this book, I can thank the LORD for the Church in which I grew up. But *something was missing*. I had a full and fulfilling life, but there was an emptiness in one important area. I didn't know what it was, but *something was missing*.

It was not a devastating emptiness. I went to school with some success. I went to work at age 15 and prospered in a series of jobs. I had family and friends. I met and married the girl who is still the love of my life. God gave us a daughter who was and is a blessing. A radio career in which I was advancing was interrupted by three years in the Air Force during the Korean War. (I am thankful for that experience — although I wouldn't want to repeat it.) I had success as a writer — but also had many disappointments in political campaigns in which I was involved.

By almost any measure, I've had a full and successful life. But with it all, *something was missing*.

I invite you to follow me through a recounting of many aspects of my life. They are paths through which the Lord lead. When I failed to follow His leading, sometimes He dragged me. At age thirty-seven, He brought me to a wonderful discovery.

Discovering what was missing brought me to complete *peace with God*. Discovering what was *missing* also brought me to a total assurance about eternity. I came to the certainty that when I draw my last breath, and am absent from this body, I will be forever in Heaven. It is nothing I could deserve or earn, because I am a sinner. But because of His love and amazing grace, Jesus, through faith, became my Lord and Savior.
Read the aspects of my "journey." Reading may help you see if something has been missing in your church and your life.

I say the truth in Christ,
I lie not, my conscience also
bearing me witness
in the Holy Ghost,
That I have great heaviness
and continual sorrow in my heart.
For I could wish that myself
were accursed from Christ
for my brethren, my kinsmen
according to the flesh.

The Apostle Paul
— Romans 9:1-3

CHAPTER 1

A GOOD CATHOLIC UPBRINGING — BUT SOMETHING WAS MISSING

Examine yourselves, whether ye be in the faith; prove your own selves. Know ye not your own selves, how that Jesus Christ is in you, except ye be reprobate.
                    —II Corinthians 13:5

I GREW UP IN A GOOD CATHOLIC HOME. For that Catholic upbringing I can still thank the Lord even though *something was missing*. Some readers may need an explanation for why I wrote the words *something was missing*. As the book unfolds, my explanation might help others determine if *something is missing* in their lives.

My parents told me that I was baptized when I was two weeks old. They faithfully took me to church on Sunday. When I was five I started Sunday school. The teachers were nuns from a neighboring parish. Our small church didn't have our own nuns or a Catholic school.

The sisters were faithful to teach us the Catechism. The Catechism was a small book which covered many essentials of the faith. It used a question and answer format. I've learned since that many non-catholic groups also had or have catechisms. These "other" catechisms have much of the same basic information as the old fashioned *Baltimore Catechism* used in Catholic churches and schools. I can still remember what I was taught through the questions and answers we memorized:

Q. Who made the world?   A. God made the world.

Q. Why did God make me?
A. God made me to know Him, love Him and serve Him

in this world and to be happy with Him forever and ever in the next.

Our Sunday school classes met before Mass each Sunday. Classes were largely based on Catechism questions and answers on essential foundational facts about God and the Catholic Church.

As a result, I've never questioned that Jesus was God, that He was born of the Virgin Mary, that He died for the sins of the world and that on the third day He arose again from the dead. I was taught and believed that God was one God who existed forever as three persons: God the Father, God the Son and God the Holy Ghost. I didn't understand the Trinity (and still don't fully) but I was told that the Trinity was one of the "mysteries" of God. I accepted that and believed it. Now, I can see the basis for the Trinity very clearly in the Bible.

I was taught and believed that there is life after death. This future life would be lived forever either in Heaven with God or in the fires of Hell. Those who died with unconfessed mortal sins would go to Hell. Hell was the place of torment made for Satan and the angels who followed Satan in his rebellion against God.

For all these basic foundational Catholic teachings, I thank the Lord. Essentially, they are the foundational Biblical facts of the Christian faith. But *something was missing.*

My Catholic upbringing, for which I can still thank the Lord, made me fully aware that there were things that were right and that there were things that were wrong. Things that were wrong were sin. Sin would separate me from God. Sin included disobeying God's Commandments and failing to be faithful to the teachings of the Church. The commandments of the Church in those days included always attending Mass on Sundays and the Holy Days of obligation, not eating meat on Fridays, and regularly saying prayers and doing good deeds. Other miscellaneous wrong thoughts, desires and deeds were considered sins.

To get to Heaven, it was needful to be a good Catholic.

A good Catholic was expected to go to Mass regularly and communion (after having first gone to confession where sins were confessed to the priest.) The priest granted forgiveness based on the individual having made a "good" confession. As a basis for forgiveness, the priest specified doing "penance." Penance was usually either a series of prayers or some other good acts specified by the priest. Doing penance, we supposed, made up in some way for sins which had been confessed and forgiven.

Foundational truths were taught and learned during my Catholic upbringing, but *something was missing.*

MY FIRST HOLY COMMUNION

I made my first communion with other boys and girls in my Sunday School class at Mass when I was six years old. We were taught (and did not question) that when the priest said certain words during the Mass over a wafer of bread that the wafer became the actual Body of the Lord Jesus Christ which we received in communion.

MEMORIZING LATIN TO BECOME AN ALTAR BOY

When I was about eight years old, our pastor, Father Leo G. Bailey, was away for six months. We were told that he visited Europe and the Vatican. While he was gone two young priests from a nearby Franciscan monastery served our parish. They were Father John Flannery and Father Paul Hatch. Almost immediately, they saw a need to train new altar boys. I was among those chosen to be trained.

Our training consisted primarily of memorizing the Latin prayers and responses used at Mass. We were never taught the English meaning of the words— but I remember some of the memorized phrases.

At the start of Mass, at the foot of the altar, the priest said, "Intro ad altare Dei," which means, "I will go to the altar of God." The altar boys, kneeling at the foot of the altar, would respond by reciting memorized Latin words:

Ad deum qui laetificat, juventutem meam.

The sequence was intermingled with some other Latin phrases and responses. Then a confession was recited in Latin by the altar boys. The first words, which after seventy years I still remember, were:

Confideor Deo, Omnipotenti, beatae Mariae semper Virgin...

From looking up the translation of that memorized Latin confession and the words which followed, I learned that the Confession, which we repeated, said:

I confess to Almighty God, to Blessed Mary ever Virgin, to Michael the Archangel, to Blessed John the Baptist, to the Holy Apostles Peter and Paul [plus a list of others named]....that I have sinned exceedingly and ask them to pray for me to the Lord our God.

Our little church did not have daily masses. Whenever there was a holy day of obligation or a funeral, the public school I attended permitted me to come to school late after serving at Mass.

My involvement as an altar boy started when I was about eight and continued until I was fifteen.

A CATHOLIC BOY SCOUT TROOP

When I was twelve, I joined Boy Scout troop #36 sponsored by St. Michael's Catholic Church in the nearby town of Hollidaysburg, Pennsylvania. Over several years I attended Boy Scout camp with the troop. We were always accompanied to camp by the pastor, Father John Cullinan. For several years Father Cullinan took a one week's vacation at a cabin my father built on a lake formed by a power dam. It was about forty miles from our home. The church janitor and I spent the week there also. The janitor did the cooking.

The only spiritual activity I recall during those weeks at the lake was the time each evening when we knelt and recited the Rosary together. The priest (a fine man) did some fishing and usually also spent some time doing the reading I believe he was required to do as a priest. I recall no instruction during that time other than Father Cullinan frequently challenging me, "John, always be a good Catholic." The two Franciscan priests who served our parish frequently issued the same challenge. But again, *something was missing*.

A RETREAT FOR BOYS AT ST. FRANCIS COLLEGE

Starting when I was ten or eleven years old, I went to retreats for young Catholic boys at St. Francis College in Loretto, Pennsylvania. The college was run by priests of the Franciscan Order.

During the retreats, a hundred or more boys started each day doing calisthenics on the practice field. Calisthenics were led by Brother Cyril. He was reported to have been a Marine before he joined the Franciscan order of monks and priests. (This was just before World War II.) A grueling time on the athletic field was followed by attendance at Mass and then breakfast.

The food was great! There was no talking at meals (except for requests to have the good family-style food passed). During each meal, one of the Franciscans read to us.

One of the books made a real impression on me. It was about the life and ministry of Prince Demetrius Gallitzin. Gallitzin was a Russian-born prince who came to America and became a priest. Starting in about 1800, Gallitzin labored as a missionary priest in the Allegheny Mountains of Pennsylvania. He used the name "Father Augustine Smith." There were believed to be only ten Catholics in 1800 in the mountainous areas of what is now Cambria County, Pennsylvania. When Gallitzin died in 1840 in Loretto, Pennsylvania, reportedly there were over 10,000 Catholics in the area as a result of his forty years of work. I was so impressed that I requested the book for Christmas to finish what we had been read.

Following meals and the regular sessions of reading, the retreat schedule had organized meetings in the church. Here, the Catholic faith was explained and we were challenged to live as "good" Catholics. But for me, *something was missing*.

LENTEN STUDIES ON THE LIFE OF CHRIST

During these growing up years my most vivid recollection of any Bible-based instruction came each year during Lent. Lent was the forty days before Easter. When our pastor, Father Bailey, came back from his earlier six months absence, he brought with him from Europe a series of 4" by 4" glass slides. The slides had beautiful full color reproductions of famous old religious paintings on the life of Christ. During Lent, we had special services every Sunday night; and some of these slides were shown. They were shown on a large, very old-fashioned carbon-arc projector which I operated.

As the slides were shown, Father Bailey explained the events in the Life of Christ as pictured in the paintings. The slide I remember most vividly was a painting of the Lord Jesus being baptized by John the Baptist. John the Baptist and the Lord Jesus were standing about knee deep in the water of the Jordan River. The painting showed John the Baptist baptizing the Lord. He used a golden cup and poured water over the Lord's head.

There were, of course, other paintings showing aspects of the Lord's life, including His birth, His miracles, and His death, burial and resurrection. His suffering was emphasized; and the glory of the empty tomb was shown.

As a boy of ten or twelve years of age, I accepted the facts. But now I've come to realize that *something was missing*. The need to personally apply the facts I had been taught was *missing*.

CHAPTER 2

A FULL-TIME JOB AT AGE 15 BRINGS SPIRITUAL CHALLENGES

O ye transgressors. Remember the former things of old; for I am God, and there is none else; I am God, and there is none like me. Declaring the end from the beginning, and from the ancient times the things that are not yet done, saying, My counsel shall stand, and I will do all my pleasure:
—Isaiah 46:8-10

JUST AFTER MY FIFTEENTH BIRTHDAY, I went to work. It was at the height of World War II. Many men were going off to war. The local radio station tired of hiring and training seventeen year olds who within a few months were called to war. On the recommendation of the high school dramatics teacher and after auditions and interviews, I was hired by the local radio station.

Starting in my sophomore year in high school and through college, I worked as an announcer forty or more hours a week, usually starting each afternoon at 3:00 p.m. Through self-study, I passed four Federal Communications Commission tests in order to be licensed as a First Class Radio Broadcast Engineer.

The radio station broadcast NBC network programs starting at 7:00 p.m. each evening. That schedule required station identifications only every half hour. Therefore, I had time to do school work. My parents insisted that I had to maintain good grades if I were to work.

Sometimes on Sundays, I worked from 7:30 a.m. until the broadcast day ended at 11:30 p.m. at night. (In those days, no one talked about eight hour days or time-and-half-time for working over forty hours a week.) The station was owned by a department store; and I was one of the higher paid employees, making 50 cents an hour. As a young Catholic, before going to work, I faithfully went to 6:00 a.m. Sunday Mass at a downtown church.

A PERSONAL GOSPEL CHALLENGE

My first real exposure to an evangelical Gospel message came at the radio station. We broadcast Jack Wyrtzen's *Word of Life* program Saturday nights from Madison Square Garden in New York. Wyrtzen, a well-known band leader, had been "saved" and started to preach. His rallies for young people filled Madison Square Garden weekly.

On Sunday mornings, the radio station broadcast the *Old Fashioned Revival Hour* with Dr. Charles E. Fuller. Both programs were received at the station on big sixteen-inch, double-sided broadcast discs. The programs featured old fashioned, Bible-based, fire-and-brimstone messages with lots of Gospel-type hymns. Because my *"ear"* was conditioned to tune out almost everything broadcast except any sound or click or squeal which wasn't supposed to be there, I never really heard the messages.

Several local pastors also had weekly programs on the station. These pastors regularly confronted me with my need of salvation. The preachers would frequently ask me if I had ever personally received Jesus Christ as my Lord and Savior. Some would ask if I was saved. Others asked if I knew for sure whether my sins were forgiven. Was I sure whether or not I was going to Heaven when I died?

Such questions made me very uncomfortable. I usually brushed them aside by replying that I was a Catholic. They would usually explain:

> *John, I'm not talking about what church you go to— that is not the issue. The important question is, have you ever really put your personal faith in Jesus Christ? Do you*

know your sins are forgiven? Do you know for sure that you are saved and going to Heaven when you die?

Back then, I didn't think anyone could be sure about going to Heaven when they died. I believed that our personal fate would be decided when we came face-to-face with the Lord Jesus Christ for the final Judgment.

TIME FOR COLLEGE

During my years at the station, we broadcast news of Pacific landings, the D-Day invasion and victory in Europe, the death of President Roosevelt and the dropping of the first atom-bomb. World War II ended just after my high school graduation.

Because of overcrowding by ex-GIs at the main campus, Penn State required students to take their freshman year at Centers in or near their home towns. I did that while continuing to work at the radio station.

For my sophomore year in electrical engineering, I moved to the main campus in State College, Pennsylvania. A newly established radio station there had an opening for a licensed broadcast engineer. I took the job, going to classes at Penn State in the daytime and working at the radio station at night. Again, there was time to study on the job. It was an ideal setup.

PHILOSOPHY CLASS SAYS "NO GOD"

A real spiritual challenge came to me personally when engineering students were required for some reason to enroll in a philosophy course. The instructor spent several weeks near the end of the semester "proving" with logic that there was no God.

Professors were perhaps more careful then than now. Therefore, the instructor spent our last day in class explaining that it is possible to prove almost anything depending on the premise from which you start. He then spent the rest of the hour giving some reasons for believing that God existed. That final one hour class didn't wipe out all the doubts created in the previous weeks of classes. As an 18-year-old away from home for the first time, there were things I wanted to do that I shouldn't, if God existed.

MAN IS MORE THAN ACCUMULATED ACCIDENTS

As a result of the philosophy class, doubts developed. But within the next two years, I concluded from looking at the world and the order in it, that it couldn't have all been the result of accumulated accidents— or evolution. There had to be a Maker and Designer; and that Maker and Creator was and is God.

I continued going to church mostly out of duty. But *something was missing.*

I went home on many weekends and with my parents I went to the Catholic Church where I had grown up. I attended, perhaps out of duty, but *something was missing.*

CHAPTER 3

MOVING TO A NEW JOB BROUGHT SOMETHING MORE IMPORTANT

House and riches are the inheritance of fathers; and a prudent wife is from the Lord ...
Whoso findeth a wife findeth a good thing, and obtaineth favour of the LORD.
—Proverbs 19:14, Proverbs 18:22

ANOTHER SURPRISE AND OPPORTUNITY came with a phone call from a man for whom I had worked at the radio station in State College, Pennsylvania. He was involved in starting a new radio station in Lewistown, Pennsylvania, about forty miles away. He wanted me to do the engineering and construction work. It paid 50% more money. I made the move. When we got the station on the air, I was the Chief Engineer and soon became the Commercial Manager also.

It was the most important move of my life. After several months of watching a young lady who often ate many of her meals in the same restaurant where I ate, we were introduced. (In those days, it wasn't regarded as proper to speak until being introduced.) Elizabeth, a social worker with the local child welfare agency, and I began spending a lot of time together. It became more serious as we met and enjoyed each others families.

Then the North Korean communists invaded South Korea. I had been classified 4-F at the end of World War II because I had what was diagnosed as a heart attack at age 16. When the Korean War started, my engineering job at the radio station should have entitled me to a deferment from the draft. However, when Uncle Sam called, I was found to be healthy and enlisted in the United States Air Force in December 1950.

Elizabeth and I were married the following summer on my first furlough. Elizabeth was Methodist. Because I was Catholic, I knew what my Catholic family expected and we were married by the priest.

MARRIED IN THE CHURCH BY THE PRIEST

We took instructions about what was required to be married in a Catholic church. The requirements were rather briefly spelled out. Looking back now I realize that *something was missing* in those instructions. It was missing for me and for her. We met with two different priests in my home town and hers. However, we were never really challenged or questioned as to what is involved in becoming or being a real Christian. *Something was missing* for both of us.

My requirement that we be married in the Church was somewhat hypocritical. I believed all the essentials and practices my Catholic training demanded. But *something was missing*.

Shortly after we were married, I was transferred to California. I was part of the 90-man cadre which opened a new west coast basic training center for the Air Force.

In the way the military does things, they soon took me, an experienced and licensed electronics engineer, and assigned me to be an Air Force Historian. Later I became the editor of the base newspaper. Both experiences were invaluable to my development as a writer and researcher.

While serving for almost three years at Parks Air Force Base we lived in Hayward, California. Both Elizabeth and I attended our own churches.

After completing my Korean War Air Force experience, I spent six months at California's San Jose State. While there I augmented my earlier several years of electrical engineering training at Penn State.

The GI-Bill support for students was meager. To support us, I worked as an announcer-engineer at radio station KEEN in San Jose, California. One of my duties required me to attend the First Baptist Church in San Jose, California where we broadcast the Sunday evening services. It was an old downtown church. The church's high square tower (it wasn't a steeple) had a blinking sign on all four sides that in red letters said, "Jesus Saves."

POWERFUL PREACHING

Pastor Sands preaching was powerful. Many people walked the aisles during the invitation at the close of each service. They were indicating, from what I understood, that they wanted to get *saved*. A week or so later many were immersed in water to be baptized.

The church custodian talked to me regularly about my need of Christ. I remember one evening before the service that we stood together on the front steps of the church. He told me that through sin, he'd ruined his life. He said, "When I finally ended up in the gutter, I trusted Christ and He gave me a new life." He added, "Young man, you need Christ also."

I laughed and said, "That's fine for you, Old Man, but I don't end up in the gutter too often."

Thus I brushed him off.

For six months every Sunday night I sat with my equipment in the church auditorium's second row broadcasting the services. Through that time I came to a sense that *those people had something I didn't have*.

But I also had a sense that if I did whatever it was they were all trying to get me to do, my life would change. I would have to give up some things. But I didn't want to make the changes which I thought would be necessary. Even here *something was missing* in the message. I didn't know then and wasn't really told that if I truly came to Christ (whatever that meant) I didn't have to give anything up. I learned later that Christ changes the desires and life of those who really come to Him.

After graduation from San Jose State, Elizabeth and I moved to St. Louis. I became the editor and general manager of *VOLT-AGE*, an electrical magazine. The position combined my engineering background with my Air Force writing experience and the Journalism major I had earned at San Jose in six months.

My wife, Elizabeth, became a founding member of the new Methodist church in the St. Louis suburb of Florissant. I started going to the local Catholic church. But still *something was missing*. Sometimes, rather than going to church, I just drove around and thought about "things." At the appropriate time, I picked Elizabeth up at the Methodist church where she became very active.

I became a father in 1958 when my daughter, Holly, was born. That caused me to start thinking about the kind of world in which Holly would grow up. I also started attending church with my wife. Although not a member, I soon became the editor of the Methodist church's weekly newsletter.

Like many churches, an annual membership drive was held to get financial pledges for the next year. My wife and I talked about how we should participate.

In the process of these discussions, we realized that we had heard somewhere about something called "tithing." Tithing as the Bible basis for giving was not preached at the church we attended. But we decided that it must have something to do with God's way of giving, so we decided to tithe. We didn't know it then, but in the Bible's Old Testament, Malachi 3:8-10 says that failing to tithe robs God. But it also promises that for those who tithe, God will open the windows of Heaven. The blessings would be so large that there would not be room to receive them.

We didn't know the promises about tithing when we started. However, within about two years, my annual income at the magazine tripled. It was another step in coming to learn that what God says in His Word is true.

We usually sat in the back row in church, so our baby daughter could stay with us. I didn't usually listen to the sermons. Mostly, I spent the time thinking about "things." When I actually started to listen, I heard some surprising things. I started to make some notes. I heard such things from the pulpit as:

The tax collector is the divine hand of God reaching into your pocket to do the things you won't do voluntarily.

All the trouble in the world is caused by these people who holler about right and wrong all the time. The world is not a court room, it's a loving home. God is not a judge, He is a loving father.

Such ideas were troubling to me. Through reading and study, I was becoming conservative in my thinking.

My wife, Elizabeth, was very active in the women's society of the church. When a Lenten Bible Study was organized in 1962, she enrolled.

The study was based on a book, titled *Basic Christian Beliefs*. Frederick C. Grant was the author. Grant taught at New York's very liberal Union Theological Seminary. He was one of the translators of the *Revised Standard Version of the Bible*. As my wife listened, she realized that the *Basic Christian Beliefs* book and the study based on it questioned or denied many of the basic Bible beliefs, including:

The Virgin Birth was ridiculed. The physical resurrection of Jesus Christ was explained away. Billy Graham's teaching that Christ's blood had to be shed to make atonement for the sin of the world was ridiculed and denied.

Elizabeth, my wife, was a lifelong Methodist but not yet a Christian in the Bible sense. However, at Syracuse University she had taken an elective Bible class in New Testament Theology. The course had given her some basic Bible knowledge. Therefore, she raised questions about some of the teachings in the *Basic Christian Beliefs* book being used in the Lenten Bible Study. As she raised questions, another woman expressed similar concerns. Discussions resulted and the pastor was recruited to get the ladies straightened out. The pastor attended the ladies study and said:

> *Let's face it, Ladies, if Jesus had known He was God, He would have crawled up on the Cross and said, "Bye, Bye, Boys, I'll see you in three days."*

My wife raised her hand and said, "Pastor, He did say He was coming back."

The pastor's response was, "He did?"

We started having on-going meetings and discussions at our home with the pastor. He had been a friend. We were about the same age. Sometimes the discussions lasted through much of the night. When the pastor finally admitted that he wasn't sure whether there was a God or not, we decided that it was time to look for another church. It was a hard decision. Almost all of my wife's out-of-home activities and friendships were in that local Methodist church.

My wife's experience in that Lenten Bible Study, and the *Basic Christian Beliefs* book and its denials of supernatural Bible events were not isolated events. Neither was the pastor's own doubting and his private questioning of the existence of God. We learned later that similar happenings had started in other mainline Protestant churches early in the 20th Century.

The questioning of supernatural events recorded in the Bible produced concerns and opposition from Bible believers and some scholars in other "mainline" denominations. Among them was J. Gresham Machen. Machen was one of the most brilliant theologians of the first half of the 20th Century. He was professor of New Testament at New Jersey's then prestigious Princeton Theological Seminary. That seminary and Machen's own Presbyterian Church were in turmoil. They were suffering from questions being raised over whether or not the Bible was the actual Word of God and whether it was without error.

Machen spoke out in lectures and in print. Finally, his work was summarized in his 1923 book, *Christianity and Liberalism*. In the book, Machen, looked at the divisions developing in Protestantism between evangelicals and the liberal deniers of traditional truth. In his book, he also acknowledged deep divisions between Rome and evangelicals. But Machen added:

> *Yet how great is the common heritage which unites the Roman Catholic Church, with its maintenance of the authority of Holy Scripture and with its acceptance of the great early creeds, to devout Protestants today! We would not obscure the difference which divides us from Rome. The gulf is indeed profound.*

That profound gulf was over how man could attain forgiveness and salvation by believing what the Lord Jesus did for us on the Cross, and then personally applying what He did to our need for a Savior. Machen continued:

> *But as profound as the gulf is, it seems almost trifling compared to the abyss which stands between us and many ministers of our own [Presbyterian] Church. The Church of Rome may represent a perversion of the Christian religion; but naturalistic liberalism [as modernist Protestantism has become] is not Christianity at all.*

On this basis the statement was made in the opening chapter of this book that I thanked the Lord for my Catholic upbringing. That upbringing rooted me in the basic fundamentals of the Christian faith— that Jesus Christ was miraculously born of the Virgin, that He was God, that He died for the sins of the world and was miraculously raised bodily from the dead on the third day.

Many of these facts were ignored or being questioned or openly denied in the Methodist Church in which my wife was brought up. Much of mainline Protestantism was also under assault by unbelieving theologians.

WE CHANGED CHURCHES

Because of what we were experiencing, we started visiting other churches. Finally, we started attending a Congregational church. It had left the Congregational denomination and became independent in the 1930s. The move was made because denominational leaders were questioning whether the Bible was the infallible Word of God and whether or not it had any errors. (The same questioning or denying of the Bible was happening those years in a number of other "mainline" Protestant denominations.) It happened particularly in more liberal denominations. They were those affiliated with or which later helped to form the Federal, National and World Councils of Churches.

At our new church, we didn't get active but heard the Word of God taught and preached every Sunday for several years. Once when I was out of town, my wife responded to the invitation to join the church. She was interviewed by the elders and was accepted into membership. She and the elders realized later that *something was missing* in the screening process.

I didn't attempt to join because as I was hearing the Bible taught and preached, I sensed that *something was missing* in me. I didn't know what it was, but I knew that *something was missing*.

SEEING THE WORLD COMMUNIST THREAT

In 1960, Elizabeth and I got involved in anti-communism studies and efforts. Castro had just seized power in Cuba (with the help of American media and the U.S. State Department). Along with conservative political activities, I started working on a book. I hoped the book would change our country and the world.

A New Job Brought Something More Important

By 1962, my wife observed that I had gotten so concerned about and involved in the problems in the world that I had lost interest in my very successful and rewarding business. She reminded me that I'd always said that if I wasn't doing the thing I most wanted to do, I couldn't be happy or truly successful. I said, "Yes, I've said that." She said, "Maybe you need to quit your job and get that book out of your system. Then we'll see what happens." She was and is both an unusual lady and good wife.

I arranged to leave my job and partial ownership of *VOLT-AGE* magazine. Initially, I wrote the speeches and helped run the 1962 campaign for the U.S. Senate in Missouri.

After losing that election, I went back to writing my book. Finishing the book took almost two years. When my "masterpiece" was complete, my wife read it. I then spent nine months revising and rewriting. Even though I had been successfully earning a living for over ten years as a writer and editor, her efforts were invaluable. The book, *None Dare Call It Treason,* became a runaway 7-million-copy bestseller. It was used by those working to nominate Senator Barry Goldwater as the Republican presidential candidate in 1964.

I became more and more involved in the effort to nominate Barry Goldwater. As I did, I came to a sense that a new man in the White House, (as desirable as that would be) wouldn't solve America's real moral or cultural problems. They were problems about which, as a young father, I was becoming more and more concerned.

None Dare Call It Treason received widespread distribution. I had opportunities to speak for Barry Goldwater around the country. (I traveled and spoke at a series of meetings, sometimes appearing with Goldwater's wife, Peggy, and other members of the family.) As I made those appearances, I started to believe and say that we wouldn't solve America's problems until we had a revival of the political and spiritual foundations on which America grew great and strong. Many people would say, "Amen!"

On a Sunday morning in September 1964, our Pastor, Norman Forge, in the congregational church preached a message detailing the numerous Old Testament prophecies of the coming of the Messiah, Jesus Christ. I'd always heard that Christ's coming was prophesied but that the Jews didn't recognize Him. But that morning I was amazed as the pastor went through dozens of specific prophecies. Those Old Testament prophesies told that the Messiah would be born of a Virgin; what His name would be; and that He would be born in Bethlehem. The prophecies described in great detail the miracles the Messiah would do and specifics about His death, His burial and His resurrection.

Psalm 22, the pastor explained, was written by David 1000 years before Christ. Even so, it pictured in great detail the crucifixion of the Lord Jesus. This was truly amazing because as Pastor Forge pointed out, the Jews, at the time when David wrote, didn't crucify. They stoned people to death. The Romans didn't even develop crucifixion as a means of execution for another 500 years.

But David in Psalm 22 wrote a detailed picture of crucifixion one thousand years before it happened. This Psalm pictured in great detail aspects of crucifixion. It even included the words, "My God, my God, why hast thou forsaken me?" which Christ would cry out on the Cross. It was all written 1000 years before it happened.

I sat in church that morning and was amazed. I said to my wife after the service, "That's the most amazing thing I've ever heard. I'm a writer. If someone were going to fake something, they'd do a more believable job of it. Every word in that Bible had to come from God." It was all written in what we call the Old Testament. It was all preserved exactly by the Jews in their Hebrew scriptures.

I had always believed *in my head* that the Bible was God's Word. In that service I came to know it also in my heart. Then

I realized that while I had read several thousand books in my life, I had never really read the Bible. The priest who gave my wife and me our premarital instructions also gave us a New Testament as a wedding gift. But I never really read it. However, once I came to know in my heart that the Bible was God's Word, I decided that as soon as the November election and my political responsibilities were over, I'd start to read the Bible every day.

November came and Barry Goldwater lost. I started to read the Bible every day. I also started to research the political effects of the widespread Christian revival of the 1700s. That revival transformed the nation and its people under the ministries of John Wesley and George Whitefield. The revival, now known as the Great Awakening, transformed America and paved the way for the Declaration of Independence and the war with great Britain.

As I read the Bible day-by-day I had no trouble with the Gospel passages about the Life of Christ and passages about sins like lying, cheating, stealing, etc. However, the theological passages in the Epistles of St. Paul were troubling for me. What did words like regeneration, propitiation, atonement, etc., mean to me?

I was also puzzled and troubled by my research on the life of John Wesley. Wesley grew up in a pastor's home in England. He went through seminary and was a missionary in America, but *something was missing.* It was thirteen years before Wesley became a *Christian,* personally trusting that Christ's work on the Cross was for *him.* Wesley came to the assurance of salvation as he heard a sermon on Martin Luther's message from Romans Chapter 4. Wesley said that after years in the ministry his heart was strangely warmed. He heard and believed the message that salvation results not from our works but through personal faith in what the death, burial and resurrection of Jesus Christ does in our lives. By faith, Wesley was saved. He was born again.

From that time on, Wesley was said to have included the words of Jesus Christ, "Ye must be born again," in every message he preached. Wesley was asked, "Mr. Wesley, why do you use the words of Jesus which said that you must be born again in every message you preach?" Wesley replied, "Because you must be born again."

God was working in my heart. That work was being done through God's Word I was reading every day. It was fortified through the work He did in and through the life of John Wesley.

Chapter 4

FEAR ABOUT AN AIRPLANE TRIP CAUSED SOMETHING TO HAPPEN

Forasmuch then as the children are partakers of flesh and blood, he also himself likewise took part of the same; that through death he might destroy him that had the power of death, that is, the devil; And deliver them who through fear of death were all their lifetime subject to bondage.
   —*Hebrews 2:14-15*

THE POPULARITY OF MY BOOK, *None Dare Call It Treason,* opened doors for a lot of public speaking engagements. One of those speaking opportunities required a trip during which I discovered what had been missing in my life.

In February 1965, I was scheduled for a series of speeches in California. The afternoon before I was to leave, my wife became concerned about all the airplane flights I was taking.

Over a seven day period I was scheduled to fly from St. Louis to Springfield, Missouri to Kansas City, to San Francisco, to Bakersfield, California, to San Diego, to Los Angeles, to Chicago, to Rockford, Illinois, and then back to Chicago and Los Angeles and San Marino, California before returning home to St. Louis. I had twelve flights in seven days.

I laughed at the concerns of my wife, saying, "Don't worry, I fly all the time." But I started to think about women's intuition. Then stories came to mind about people who missed a flight for some reason and thereby avoided dying when a plane crashed. (A few months earlier, a couple from Cape Girardeau, Missouri had won a trip to Japan in a sales contest. At the last minute they couldn't go and gave the tickets to friends. The plane crashed on Mount Fujiama in Japan. All were killed.)

As I considered the concerns of my wife (and my own growing fears), I wondered if perhaps God was warning me.

During the middle of the night, I awoke and stood in my darkened living room. Could I skip one stop and get a train to make my first speech in San Francisco? That wouldn't work. I considered canceling the trip. But I was too embarrassed to say I was afraid to fly. I couldn't lie and say I was sick. With all my Bible reading I was trying to live right.

For the first time in my life, I realized that if one of those planes crashed I was in serious trouble. I'd always known that I was a sinner. But I never thought I was bad enough to go to Hell. As a Catholic, I also had the assurance that if I did die with unconfessed sins I could go to Heaven, after a time of cleansing in Purgatory.

That night in the darkened living room, I realized that if one of the planes went down, I was going to Hell if God gave me what I deserved. I said, "Lord, I don't know why you'd send a plane down with me on it, but if you do I'm going to have to trust that Christ did die for *my* sins."

I went back to bed and slept the rest of the night. In the morning, I went to the airport. I was scared to death, but kept saying to myself, "Lord, I'm in your hands."

The first flight took me to Springfield, Missouri. I was attending the Republican Lincoln Day statewide observance. I had a role in the meeting and a lot of my friends were there. I was a member of the Republican State Committee. As a member of the Missouri delegation, I had attended the 1964 Republican convention in San Francisco which nominated Barry Goldwater.

I went to the smoke-filled back room with my friends. But things were different. The jokes didn't seem funny anymore. The wheeling and dealing in which I always had a part didn't seem important. I didn't stay for the afternoon meeting and the banquet that evening. I got an earlier plane to Kansas City where I waited for my early morning flight to San Francisco.

On the flight to San Francisco, I found myself praying. It wasn't a matter of just reciting prayers I'd learned; I was talking to God. He was no longer a judge to be feared. He was like my Father; and I wanted to talk with Him. I later learned from the Bible what was happening to me. Of newly saved Christians, *Galatians 4:6* says:

And because ye are sons, God hath sent forth the Spirit of his Son into your hearts, crying, Abba, Father.

On the flight, I read the Bible as I had been doing every morning for several months. Suddenly, the Bible was like a new book. I wasn't seeing so much of what I should do or shouldn't do. Instead, I was seeing what the Lord *had done for me.* The Bible came alive to me for the first time. Later I learned that *I Corinthians 2:14* tells what was happening to me and why. It says:

But the natural man [man in his natural, unsaved, sinful state] receiveth not the things of the Spirit of God: for they are foolishness unto him: neither can he know them, because they are spiritually discerned.

When a person truly trusts that the Lord Jesus died for his or her own personal sins, the Holy Spirit comes into the new Christian's life and gives the new birth. The same Spirit who gives that newly-born Christian an understanding of God's Word also inspired the Scripture writers to write the Bible. Only He can make it understandable.

When I arrived in California, some of the people who met me at the airport started talking about how they had recently been saved. I usually tried to stay away from such folks. Otherwise, they'd soon be asking, "Are you saved? Do you know the Lord?"

But now I didn't try to get away from these new friends. They were the nicest people I'd ever met. I found myself really loving to be with them. That's another Biblical confirmation of salvation— of the new birth. *I John 3:14* says:

> *We <u>know</u> that we have passed from death unto life, because we love the brethren. He that loveth not his brother abideth in death.*

The same things happened with other people I met as I went from San Francisco to Bakersfield and then to San Diego. I was a new person. I was, although I didn't know it yet. *II Corinthians 5:17-18a* describes the transformation which takes place when an individual sinner trusts or believes *on* Christ and not just *about* Him. The Scripture says:

> *Therefore if any man be in Christ, he is a new creature: old things are passed away; behold, all things are become new. And all things are of God, who hath reconciled us to himself by Jesus Christ, <u>and hath given to us the ministry of reconciliation;</u>*

Once we have trusted Christ He gives us a desire to see others know Him as we do. That happened to me very quickly. The following Thursday, I had to fly from San Diego to Los Angeles to Chicago and then ultimately to Rockford, Illinois. In Rockford, I was scheduled to speak to a meeting of the *Daughters of the American Revolution*. After that speech I was to fly quickly back to Los Angeles. (I had a really goofed up schedule that week.)

This was when airlines first started assigning seats to people. As I got into my assigned place on the aisle a man showed up and crawled across me to his window seat. He introduced himself. We had breakfast (they still served meals in those days). Then I opened my Bible. I didn't read for very long, before he asked, "Is that your Bible?" I answered, "Yes, it's my Bible. I've been reading it lately; and it's just like God talking to me."

The man started to cry. He told me that he had been in California to bury his father. He was realizing that it would also happen to him someday. The scripture says:

> *It is appointed unto men once to die, but after this the judgment.*

He started telling me about some of his World War II experiences. Then he said, "You get into business and you have to start cutting some corners to get along. Men can understand, but how am I going to explain it to God?"

I told him that none of us can answer for ourselves. I pointed to my Bible and said:

It says in here somewhere that none of us can answer for ourselves. That's why the Lord Jesus had to come to earth. On the Cross, He took all of our personal sins upon Himself and died for them. He answered for us by taking the punishment we all deserve. If you believe that, the Bible says that you'll be OK.

In talking to that troubled man on the airplane I came to realize why I was experiencing all these new things. I had found the *"something"* which had been missing for so many years.

I had been taught and always believed that Christ died for the sins of the world, was buried and rose again. What I had been taught and believed didn't do me any good, until I saw that He died, not just for the sins of the world, but for ME personally.

We have to see ourselves as LOST before we can be saved. The lost individual must also want a new life. (The Bible calls this desire *repentance*.) It is necessary because God doesn't save those who are "pretty good." The Lord Jesus in *Luke 19:10* said:

I come to seek and save that which was <u>lost.</u>

How does an individual come to the place of knowing that he or she *personally* deserves to go to Hell? It comes as a result of seeing ourselves *personally* as God sees us. The Bible tells us how He actually sees each of us. In the Old Testament, *Psalm 53:2-3* says:

God looked down from heaven upon the children of men, to see if there were any that did understand, that did seek God. Every one of them is gone back: they are altogether become filthy; there is none that doeth good, no, not one.

That is very clear. As a result of the sinful life we inherited from Adam, we are all sinners. We are born sinners. We want our own way. Any parent knows that we don't have to teach children to be bad. In spite of all the teaching, training and discipline, a child still wants its own way. Obviously, our children are born as sinners. Each of us was also.

In the New Testament, St. Paul's Epistle to the church at Rome spells out the grim picture. *Romans Chapter 3*, starting in verse 9, contrasts us with the Jews who have broken God's law and pagans who have never been given God's law.

The passage says:

What then? are we better than they? No, in no wise: for we have before proved both Jews and Gentiles [Pagans], that they are all under sin; As it is written, There is <u>none</u> righteous, no, not one:

This is very blunt. But it is God's evaluation of what we are. The result in our lives is described in *Romans 3:17-18* which says:

And the way of peace have they not known: There is no fear of God before their eyes.

Because I had been reading the Bible for several months, I came to know that I was LOST. Fortunately, God loves us too much to leave us that way. His Word didn't just show me my lost condition. The Bible also presents God's answer for my need.

Because we are sinners, there is no hope for us, apart from what God the Father did when He sent His Son, the Lord Jesus, to earth. Christ came, lived a sinless life, went to the Cross and died in our place. He took the punishment we all deserve and was raised again from the dead on the third day to be the new life of those who believe and put their trust in Him.

The Apostle Paul in his Epistle to the church at Ephesus sums up the message this way in *Ephesians 2:8-10*:

> *For by grace are ye saved through faith; and that not of yourselves: it is the gift of God: Not of works, lest any man should boast. For we are his workmanship, created in Christ Jesus unto good works, which God hath before ordained that we should walk in them.*

Because He loves us, God saves those who put their personal trust in the blood Christ shed on the Cross for the salvation of sinners. When the Lord died on the Cross, all of our sins were in the future, but He, being God, knew about them and took them all. On the Cross, He cried out concerning the work the Father sent Him to do, saying:

> *It is finished. (John 19:30)*

Doing good works cannot make us good enough for God. Does this eliminate the need for us to do good works? No! Because of what God has done in providing salvation for us as a free gift, we should go on to serve Him. We serve not for what we might get, but out of gratitude for what He has already done in saving us from our sin.

When Saul of Tarsus met the resurrected Lord Jesus on the road to Damascus, Saul believed. He was given a new life and a new name. He became the Apostle Paul. His first words, as recorded in *Acts 9:6*, were:

> *Lord, what wilt thou have me to do?*

Those words should be our cry once we believe. Those should be our first words each new day.

As far as I know, I wasn't able to help that troubled man seated beside me on that airplane. To my knowledge, he didn't come to Christ and salvation that morning. He cried most of the way until we landed in Chicago. I've prayed for him for years.

On the airplane that morning, as I tried to help him, I came to an assurance of the salvation I had received when I cried out to God that night a week earlier.

If you have read this far in my book, *Something Was Missing,* the question for you is:

> *Have you ever come to see yourself as a lost sinner, deserving of Hell? Once the individual sees his or her need for <u>a</u> Savior, Christ will become <u>the</u> Savior of the person who believes that Christ died on the Cross, not just for the sins of the world, but for the individual's personal sins.*
>
> *Do you believe that Christ died on the Cross for all of <u>your</u> sins? Do you believe that He arose from the dead? Are you willing to invite Him into your life? Are you willing to have Him do in and through you whatever He desires to do. If you are willing, you can ask Him to come into your life and take charge as your Savior and Lord.*

Believing is not a feeling. It is not an emotion. Believing results from a decision— a decision to trust what God says that He did for you. Believing is taking Him at His Word.

Once we believe, Psalm 66:16 says we are to tell others about the changes God made when we believed. It says:

> *Come and hear, all ye that fear God, and I will declare what He hath done for my soul.*

Man's soul is composed of (1) our minds where we think, (2) our emotions where we feel, and (3) our wills where we make decisions.

The new birth changes the soul. The new birth changes how the individual feels in his emotions, how he thinks in his mind and the decisions he makes in his will.

As II Corinthians 5:17 says, the individual who trusts Christ and is born again becomes a new person.

Can you remember that time when your faith in Christ transformed the way that you think and changed the way that you feel and the way you decide things?

CHAPTER 5

MY NEW LIFE BROUGHT NEW RESPONSIBILITIES

If any of you lack wisdom, let him ask of God, that giveth to all men liberally, and unbraitheth not; and it shall be given him. But let him ask in faith, nothing wavering. For he that wavereth is like a wave of the sea driven by the wind and tossed.
— *James 1:5-6*

IN FEAR, I CALLED OUT TO THE LORD in my dark living room that night. I wasn't consciously making a spiritual decision. I was just concerned about what would happen to me if a plane crashed. Circumstances brought me to a place where I couldn't look to anyone but the Lord so I cried out to Him.

As spelled out in the previous chapter, all sorts of new things started to happen. However, it was a full week before I realized that I'd actually trusted the Lord Jesus for salvation that night for the first time. I'd believed *on* Him rather than just believing *about* Him. Since I was a very young child I had always believed about Him. That night in the dark, I believed that what He had done on the Cross was for me *personally*. As a result, I was saved. I'd been born again.

Things started happening when I *trusted* the Lord rather than just believing about Him. Even before I realized what happened to me, I started talking to the Lord (instead of just reciting prayers). I had a new understanding of the Bible. Also, I found myself loving Christians. This was all new to me. What was new to me was that I was now a new-born Christian. Actually, to be a real Christian, it is necessary to be *born again*. The Lord Jesus said in John 3:3-7, "Ye *must* be born again." There are no exceptions.

Realizing what had happened to me made me face some new responsibilities. I realized that my wife, although she was always a serious church-goer, probably needed to be saved also. I hesitated to tell her. (I knew what I had always thought about people who talked about being "saved" and being "born again").

She says now that I chased her around with a Bible for a month. I didn't tell her about my salvation. I didn't explain that I'd found the *something* which had been missing in my life. That *something* was the need to trust and believe that it was for *me* He died. That opened the door to salvation.

My wife and I had both been through some difficult times. For almost four years we'd been deeply involved in losing the vitally important 1964 presidential election. What made it even more difficult for my wife was seeing the name, "Stormer," in headlines for weeks. Our name appeared along with words like *lies, fraud* and *deceit*. Liberals didn't like the message of my book, *None Dare Call It Treason*. The reactions didn't surprise me. In writing what became a widely distributed book about the influence of communism in our basic institutions, I expected the attacks. But what she saw as the unfairness of it was harder for her.

Rather than telling her exactly what had happened to me when I trusted Christ that night in the dark, I'd just say, "A few weeks ago I put it all in the Lord's hands and He's made it all OK." Her response was, "Certainly, everyone knows that — but what are we going to do?"

In March 1965, Sunday came and I wanted to go to church. Elizabeth didn't go with me that day. So I took Holly, our seven-year-old daughter, and went without her. That morning, a couple, who were close personal and political friends, went forward at the close of the service. The woman was making a public acknowledgement that she had believed and been saved a few weeks earlier. Responding to the pastor's invitation, her husband was publicly expressing a desire to be saved. I reported the news excitedly when I got home from church. My wife was not impressed.

I had an appointment to attend a meeting that evening. Before I left, Elizabeth had locked herself in the bedroom. It was the only time that happened, before or since, in our now 58 years of marriage.

But she locked herself up with the Bible and started reading the *Gospel of St. John*. I am now sure that the Lord arranged that. The *Gospel of St. John.* was written so individuals can believe and get eternal life. Chapter 20 follows the nineteen previous chapters which record the works and promises of Jesus Christ. John 20:30-31 says:

> *And many other signs truly did Jesus in the presence of his disciples, which are not written in this book: But these are written, that ye might believe that Jesus is the Christ, the Son of God; and that believing ye might have life through his name.*

John wrote his Gospel to help people come to saving faith in Jesus Christ. John 3:16 is one of the many promises the Lord made in the Gospel of John. It may be the best known verse in the Bible. John 3:16 says:

> *For God so loved the world, that he gave his only begotten Son, that whosoever believeth in him should not perish, but have everlasting life.*

Many promises made by the Lord Jesus in the Gospel of John also concern salvation and everlasting life. Others promise deliverance from condemnation and judgment:

> *Verily, verily, I say unto you, He that heareth my word, and believeth on him that sent me, hath everlasting life, and shall not come into condemnation; but is passed from death unto life (John 5:24).*

> *For God sent not his Son into the world to condemn the world; but that the world through him might be saved. He that believeth on him is not condemned: but he that believeth not is condemned already, because he hath not believed in the name of the only begotten Son of God (John 3:17-18).*

When these words of the Lord Jesus are read, it is helpful if the reader particularly notes the words "condemned," "believe" and "everlasting life." Ask, "How do these words apply to me personally?"

John 3:36 is another verse which was written to bring people to faith and everlasting life. It says:

> *He that believeth on the Son <u>hath</u> everlasting life: and he that believeth not the Son shall not see life; but the wrath of God abideth on him.*

Note the tense of the underlined word "hath." That present tense verb indicates that the believer *has* everlasting life. Everlasting life is not something the believer will receive sometime in the future. Grammar and verb tenses are important in interpreting and understanding God's promises.

John 8:24 is another warning. The Lord Jesus says:

> *I said therefore unto you, that ye shall die in your sins: for if ye believe not that I am he, ye shall die in your sins.*

Back to Elizabeth. That night, in the locked bedroom, my wife read the first ten chapters of the *Gospel of John*. In *Chapter 10*, the Lord Jesus in verse 9 said:

> *I am the door [of the sheep] by me if any man enter in, he shall be saved....I am come that they might have life, and that they might have it more abundantly. I am the good shepherd: the good shepherd giveth his life for the sheep.*

When applied personally, those verses have both immediate and eternal promise. A few verses later Elizabeth read where Jesus explained:

> *Therefore doth my Father love me, because I lay down my life, that I might take it again. No man taketh it from me, but I lay it down of myself. I have power to lay it down, and I have power to take it again.*

At that point my wife realized that if Jesus had the power to lay His life down, and then take it up again, He must be God. She had never been taught or brought to see that Jesus Christ was God in any Methodist churches in which she grew up. *Something had been missing* in her upbringing. It was *something different* from what had been missing for me. Both *missing truths* are necessary for salvation and a new life.

When my wife realized that Jesus was God, she already knew she was a sinner. She dropped to her knees beside the bed and asked the Lord to take her life. She says that the Lord spoke to her in her heart and said, "Seek my guidance in all things."

John 6:37 promises:

> *All that the Father giveth me shall come to me; and him that cometh to me I will in no wise cast out.*

Romans 10:10 and Romans 10:13 says:

> *For with the heart man believeth unto righteousness; and with the mouth confession is made unto salvation.... For whosoever shall call upon the name of the Lord shall be saved.*

When I got home later that evening, she greeted me with the news that she had been saved. Hallelujah! During those four weeks since the Lord saved me, we had been two different people. It had been difficult. I was a new person and she wasn't. It put a wall between us. When she got saved, the wall came down.

NOW THERE WERE LOTS OF DECISIONS TO MAKE

For several years, we had gone to a church where the Bible was faithfully preached. But through conservative and political activities, I had come to know that there were many different kinds of churches which appeared to believe the Bible. There were Baptist churches. There was a small Evangelical Methodist denomination. One of those churches was the first place in which I was invited to speak a month after I was saved.

Others I knew to be Bible-believing included Bible churches and Nazarene churches. I had ongoing contact with a Lutheran pastor who was true to the Bible and preached salvation through faith in Jesus Christ.

Over several years before and after salvation I had developed a relationship with Dr. Carl McIntire and the Bible Presbyterian church. For many years, Dr. McIntire had daily broadcasts on hundreds of radio stations across America. He opposed communism and its influence in the liberal National and World Councils of Churches and the Baptist World Alliance.

In listening to him for several years, I had become impressed that before dealing with the problems of communism, Carl McIntire started every half hour daily broadcast with ten or more minutes presenting the Gospel. He also defended the Bible against the attacks made by liberals in mainline Protestant denominations. As a young man, McIntire had been a student of Dr. J. Gresham Machen, the early Princeton Seminary theologian, quoted in a previous chapter.

So I was familiar with groups of churches which had broken with their original mainline Protestant denominations over the issue of whether the Bible was truly the Word of God. As they believed the Bible was the Word of God, they believed it was therefore without error. These groups preached salvation through personal faith in the Lord Jesus Christ and His death, burial and resurrection.

Once I knew that the Lord had saved me, I knew that I should be in the church where God wanted me to be. The first words of the Apostle Paul, once he had met and believed on the Lord Jesus, are recorded in Acts 9:6. They were:

Lord, what wilt thou have me to do?

Those were the words I applied once I knew that the Lord had saved me. I knew that there were a number of Bible-believing churches. However, I surmised that their different names indicated that they all had some differences which must be important.

As I investigated, I found that there were differences between churches and groups over baptism. They differed over what baptism meant, over who could be baptized and how it was to be done. There were differences between the various church denominations, including Catholic, over the Lord's Supper (communion).

There were differences among some churches over whether a person who had been saved and given eternal life through believing on Jesus could ever lose it. If through sin a believer could lose the eternal life received through faith, would it have been eternal? I needed to find out what the differences were and determine which church was closest to what the Bible actually taught.

Finding the church where God would have us to worship and serve the Lord and raise our seven-year-old daughter was crucial. We loved the very large church where we had attended for three years. The Bible was preached. The people were kind and loving. Many were people we came to know and love in the three years we attended there. Some were people we had worked with politically. But it would have been easy to get lost in a big church where we could evade our responsibilities to the Lord.

The Lord moved us to a small independent Baptist church where the Bible was taught and preached. There was a vigorous program of outreach to lost people who needed Christ. This was important as we had many political and conservative friends who needed Christ.

This was all good, but I had a problem. The Baptist Church required that before an individual who had been saved could join the church, baptism (immersion) in water was required. I struggled. I was baptized when sprinkled with water as a baby. I resisted the requirement that I be "baptized" again. I told the preacher that he was making it harder to join the church than it is to get to Heaven. He wasn't impressed.

As will be explained in a later chapter, through studying every verse in the Bible concerning baptism, I came to see that immersion in water *after salvation* is the Bible way of baptism.

Being baptized that way was a public testimony that I believed that Jesus Christ died for me, was buried and then raised again the third day to be my new life. I was baptized, joined the church and became active in the outreach of the church, including witnessing to others.

Not only did I see my wife come to Christ, but a number of other politically active friends — including husbands and wives and older children — were also saved.

CHAPTER 6

A Question and Challenge:
"JOHN: WHY DID YOU LEAVE THE ONE TRUE CHURCH?"

But sanctify the Lord God in your hearts: and be ready always to give an answer to every man that asketh you a reason of the hope that is in you, with meekness and fear.
—*1 Peter 3:15*

I NEVER MADE IT A SECRET that I was born and raised as a Catholic. Neither did I make a big deal about no longer being Catholic. Friends who knew responded in various ways. Some said, "That's interesting." Others came to Christ themselves. A few said that I had "flipped" over religion.

One longtime friend, a very committed and dedicated Catholic conservative activist, tried for years to get me to return to the church in which I had grown up.

After twenty years of such effort, in 1988, he wrote me a very kind, but challenging, personal letter. His letter started by recalling our association and friendship for many years. He complimented me on my conservative efforts for which he also labored. (He was one of those who placed a significant advance order for *None Dare Call It Treason*. He and others like him helped me get the book in print.) His letter presented this challenge:

> *It is my understanding that you relinquished your Roman Catholic Faith. Tell me: Why did you, John?*

Responding gave me an opportunity to really share how I finally learned what was *missing* in my good Catholic upbringing. His challenge also allowed me to pass along what I learned in years of research about the important differences between Catholic dogma, ritual and practice and what the Bible teaches.

His letter was very challenging. His letter covered his long and rich life in inspiring and touching ways. The education, training and discipline that old-fashioned Catholic nuns built into his life had made him a man of unusual character and achievement. He was one of the finest men I've ever known.

He was about twenty years older than I. His letter recounted the intensive character training he attributed to his Catholic upbringing. My father's life manifested similar stellar character. (My generation's schooling had basically missed much of the emphasis on building character from which both my father and my friend had profited.)

My friend's letter and his personal life and character were challenging. However, character is no substitute for a true personal relationship with Christ. That relationship comes through personal faith in the Lord Jesus and what He did through His death on the Cross, His Burial and His resurrected life. The salvation and new life which results in an individual through faith cannot be produced through character and good works, as important as they both are.

Whether my Catholic friend, now gone from this life, had that personal saving relationship with Jesus Christ, I don't know. I wanted to explore the doctrinal foundation of his Catholic faith through my letter which responded to his challenge. I wanted to see whether he had ever come to find and believe what I knew had been missing in my Catholic upbringing and life. He never gave me the opportunity. He refused to discuss the 48-page letter I wrote in response to his question and challenge.

In answering his question, I had to make something plain to him. In his letter and challenge, he said:

It is my understanding that you relinquished your Roman Catholic Faith. Tell me: Why did you, John?

I started my 48-page letter saying, "In my growing up, I believed all the right things *about* Jesus Christ. But I now know that I never came to true faith *in* the Lord Jesus in the way which produces salvation, forgiveness and eternal life." I tried to make my friend understand that even though I was born and baptized Catholic, I never really had a true faith in Christ to relinquish. A very essential *something was missing* in all that I was taught and believed.

My friend's letter, on page 3, said:

> *Jesus Christ founded ONE church. It was catholic [meaning universal] and apostolic. When Christ ascended into heaven, a packet of faith was complete. Nothing needed to be added or subtracted. He did not leave us a faith which needed to evolve. It was always there, absolute and immutable.*

With that statement I agreed wholeheartedly (then and now). The Church the Lord started is immutable — it was and is unchanging. My friend's statement gave me the basis for explaining why I had left what my friend considered to be (and what I had once been taught) was the one true church.

In the following chapters of this book, the current practices, rituals and teaching of the Catholic Church as spelled out in its Catechisms will be examined and compared with the teaching of the Word of God. I needed to see if the Church the Lord started had changed in any way.

Obtaining the Catholic Catechism was part of my restudying the Catholic faith. It was part of my search for God's church after I came to a true saving faith in Jesus Christ 45 years ago. The "official" Catechism then was the *Confraternity Edition, Baltimore Catechism, No. 3*. The author was Father Francis J. Connell, Catholic University, Washington, D.C. It had the imprimaturs of Edwin V. O'Hara, Archbishop of Kansas City, and Francis Cardinal Spellman of New York. The Catechism said:

> *It is unthinkable that an institution established by God for the salvation of souls could lead men into error and turn them away from God. If the Church could and did err in matters of faith or morals, it would not be a true teacher; it would fail in its ministry of sanctification and would not lead men to salvation but would be responsible for their condemnation....It would be impossible for Christ to be with the official teachers of the Church and permit them to teach error.*

I agreed then and now with that statement from the Catholic Catechism. In my 48-page reply to my friend's challenge to explain why I had left the Catholic Church, I said that I hoped we could both agree with that Catechism statement. The Catholic Catechism said that if the Catholic Church departed in any way from what was taught and practiced in the early church, the authenticity of the *evolving* or changing church and its practices would be in question. In his letter, my friend stated that God's true church could not evolve or change.

My reply suggested that there must be an agreement on some ground rules. What each of us thinks or what some priest teaches or even that on which we might both agree is not important *unless it is God's way*. So then the question becomes: How do we determine God's Will and Way.

TRUTH: WHAT IS IT AND HOW CAN WE KNOW IT?

The place to start must be *The Holy Bible*. The Bible was written for us by the Apostles and disciples. They wrote as they were moved by the Spirit of God to remember and write what the Lord Jesus had taught them. The night before He went to the Cross, He promised them in John 14:26:

> *...the Comforter, which is the Holy Ghost, whom the Father will send in my name, he shall teach you all*

things, and bring all things to your remembrance, whatsoever I have said unto you.

So the Holy Spirit came to direct the Lord's Apostles and disciples in writing the exact words God wanted in the Bible.

The Catholic Church accepts *The Holy Bible*, the Written Word, as infallible. Pope Pius XII, in his *Encyclical on The Reading of the Sacred Scripture,* said of the Bible:

> *This Heaven-sent treasure, Holy Church considers as the most precious source of doctrine on faith and morals.*

In his *Encyclical on Reading the Sacred Scripture,* Pius XII quoted II Timothy 3:16 which says:

> *All scripture is inspired by God and is useful for teaching, for reproving, for correcting, for instructing in justice [righteousness].*

This is another area where fundamental Protestants and Baptists agree with the *official* teaching of the Catholic Church concerning the Bible.

In the chapters which follow, the current practices, rituals and teachings of the Catholic Church, as defined in their authoritative Catechisms will be examined. They will be compared with the teachings and practices of the early church as recorded and spelled out in the Book of Acts in the Bible and in the Epistles written to those early churches by Apostles Peter, Paul, James and John. The Book of Acts, written by Luke under the inspiration of the Holy Spirit, is God's record of how the early church operated. The Epistles, written in the First Century to newly forming churches and people by the Apostles, had the goal of keeping new Christians doctrinally straight. In some cases, the Epistles were written to make corrections where a local church had gone astray in some way.

With that as background, the next chapters will explore apparent conflicts between the Bible and the teachings and practices set forth in the Catholic Catechisms. When some traditions and teachings of the Catholic Church appeared to be in conflict with the Word of God, I realized that I needed to find and be in the church where God wanted me to be.

CHAPTER 7

HOW HAS THE LORD'S EARLY CHURCH BEEN CHANGED?

Study to shew thyself approved unto God, a workman that needeth not to be ashamed, rightly dividing (applying) the word of turth.
—1I Timothy 2:15

ONCE I WAS SAVED, I DIDN'T JUST WANT A CHURCH THAT SUITED ME . Instead I wanted the church of God's choice. At that point I had been away from attending the Catholic church regularly for almost ten years. During those years, the Latin mass was largely put aside by VATICAN II. There were many other changes as well.

But even so, my early training said that the Catholic Church was the "one true church." That caused me to take a new fresh look once I was saved. I wanted to please God no matter where it took me.

My friend, on page 3 of his letter, challenged me to explain why I was no longer a Catholic. His statement on the Church was published in the previous chapter. It is worthy of being repeated here. My friend wrote:

> Jesus Christ founded ONE church. It was catholic [meaning universal] and apostolic. When he ascended into heaven, the packet of faith was complete. Nothing needed to be added or subtracted. He did not leave us a Faith which needed to evolve. It was always there, absolute and immutable.

With that statement I agreed wholeheartedly. But his statement prompts the question, "How can we find out what the Church the Lord founded looks like?"

The message and practices of the early church established by the Apostles are recorded and preserved for us in the Book of Acts and the Epistles. When the twenty-seven books of the New Testament were complete, there was no need for anything to be added or subtracted. The Scriptures close with a solemn warning to anyone who would add or subtract from the Word of God.

> *For I testify unto every man that heareth the words of the prophecy of this book, If any man shall add unto these things, God shall add unto him the plagues that are written in this book:*
>
> *And if any man shall take away from the words of the book of this prophecy, God shall take away his part out of the book of life...(Revelation 22:18-19)*

As my friend said:

> *He did not leave us a Faith which needed to evolve. It was always there, absolute and immutable.*

The Bible gives us the inspired record of the Church in which the Lord had the Apostles serve. We can know what it preached and what its practices were. That inspired record is the *Book of Acts*. Acts was written by St. Luke under the inspiration of the Holy Spirit. The Bible's Book of Acts covers a period of about 32 years, from the Ascension of the Lord Jesus to Heaven (Acts 1:8-9) to Luke's arrival in Rome with the Apostle Paul about 30 years later (Acts 28).

From the *Book of Acts* and the Epistles of the Apostles, Paul, Peter, James and John, we get a very good picture of the theology and practice of the Church established by the Lord Jesus. Of that early Church, my friend wrote:

> *Jesus Christ founded ONE church....Nothing needed to be added or subtracted. He did not leave us a Faith which needed to evolve. It was always there, absolute and immutable.*

How Has the Lord's Early Church Been Changed?

That is true. But when I started my own study of the Bible record of the early church, why did I find so many changes between the Bible and Catholic teaching? Why did I find so much evidence of an *evolving* over the centuries? Why did I find so many crucial areas where the teaching of the Catholic Church and its *traditions* appear to be in actual conflict with the clear teaching of the Bible?

Such a charge demands documentation. Therefore, the chapters which follow will explore, the conflicts found between the Bible and the *traditions,* doctrine, ritual and practice of today's Catholic Church.

These conflicts and contradictions are in about ten primary areas. The conflicts between the Bible and Catholic teaching and practice include: (1) To whom should we pray, (2) The making of statues, (3) Forbidding priests to marry, (4) The thousand years of forbidding Catholics to eat meat on Fridays, (5) The way of salvation, (6) purgatory, (7) the question of who should be baptized and when and how it should be done; (8) The meaning and merits of the Mass, (9) Papal authority, and (10) Whether or not Catholics can be saved and know it now.

TO WHOM SHOULD WE PRAY?

Catholic tradition, teaching and practice include praying to (or through) the Virgin Mary and the saints.

The *Baltimore Catechism,* Lesson 17, entitled, *"Honoring the Saints, Relics and Images,"* asks, "How can we honor the saints (Q 216)?" The answer is threefold:

> *We can honor the saints: first, by imitating their holy lives; <u>second, by praying to them</u>; third, by showing respect to their relics and images.*

> *The Catechism's question and answer which follows expounds on this issue, asking, "When we pray to the saints what do we ask them to do?" The Catechism answer for Catholics, young and old, is:*

> *When we pray to the saints we ask them to offer their prayers for us.*

This teaching of the Catechism makes saints "go-betweens" or "mediators" between God and man. It says that we are to pray to saints so they can pray to God for us. This sounds nice but is in conflict with the Bible and the teaching of the Lord Jesus on prayer in several ways. The Bible teaching on prayer merits examination:

(1) When the disciples asked Jesus to teach them to pray, the Lord said, "After this manner therefore pray ye: Our Father which art in Heaven...."

Jesus taught people to pray directly to their Heavenly Father. In John 14:6, the Lord cautioned that individuals could reach the Father only through Him. The Lord said:

> *...no man comes unto the Father but by me.*

This is why St. Paul in I Timothy 2:5 taught:

> *...there is one God, and one Mediator between God and men, the man Christ Jesus.*

On this basis alone we can come to the Father *only* through Jesus Christ. The teaching in the Catechism uses saints and the Virgin Mary as the "go-betweens" through whom we come to God. However, the Bible says clearly that the Lord Jesus is the *only* mediator or intercessor between man and God, the Heavenly Father.

We have direct access to God through Jesus Christ <u>and Him only</u>. He is our intercessor and we need no other. Hebrews 7:25 says:

> *Therefore He is able <u>at all times</u> to save those who come to God <u>through Him</u> since He lives always to make intercession for them.*

The Lord Jesus Christ commanded us to come to Himself. In Matthew 11:28 He said:

> *Come unto me, all ye that labour and are heavy laden, and I will give you rest.*

The Bible clearly invites and commands us to come directly to the Lord Himself. That being so, why try to approach God, as Church *tradition* teaches, through the Virgin Mary or someone that the Church has designated as a saint?

REPETITIVE PRAYERS

Repetitious prayers, like the *Rosary*, appear to violate the caution of the Lord Jesus in the *Sermon on the Mount*. In Matthew 6:7, The Lord Jesus said:

> *But when ye pray, use not vain repetitions, as the heathen do: for they think that they shall be heard for their much speaking.*

Catholics pray the *Rosary* either individually, in families or in groups. Rosary beads are used to keep track of the number of times certain prayers are repeated. The Catholic Hail Mary prayer is repeated numerous times, interspersed with repetitions of the Lord's Prayer and mentions of mysteries which can be a basis for meditation. The Hail Mary, the basic prayer, is repeated twenty-five or more times in saying the *Rosary*.

The *Catholic Encyclopedia* says the origin of the Hail Mary prayer is unknown. It adds that it is generally believed to have originated with St. Dominic in the 13th Century. It was incorporated into the *Rosary* in the 15th Century. The use of beads as a basis for keeping track of prayers being recited is a practice found also in Buddhist, Islam, and other religions today and in antiquity.

When the disciples asked the Lord, in Matthew 6 and Luke 11, to teach them to pray He didn't give them versions of the Lord's Prayer to memorize and repeat. Instead, He said, *"After this manner, therefore, pray ye..."* He was giving them a blueprint or guide for prayerful meditating and praying— not a prayer to repeat.

THE BIBLE AND THE MAKING OF STATUES

In the Catechism lesson quoted earlier, Catholics are taught to honor the saints "*by showing respect to their relics and images.*" This teaching is in direct conflict with the 2nd Commandment [The 2nd Commandment is part of the 1st Commandment in the Catholic version]. It says:

> *Thou shalt not make unto thee any graven image, or any likeness of any thing that is in heaven above, or that is in the earth beneath, or that is in the water under the earth. Thou shalt not bow down thyself to them, nor serve them: for I the Lord thy God am a jealous God...*

As a young Catholic I was taught to tell people who questioned our praying to "idols" that we were not praying to them. The statues were "helps" for our prayer life. I didn't think I was praying to a statue but to the saint which the statue represented. I didn't know and never checked to see that the *Second Commandment* doesn't just forbid bowing down to or praying to graven or carved images. It forbids making them!

Catholic *tradition*, teaching and practice on the making of statues conflicts with one of the Ten Commandments.

FORBIDDING PRIESTS TO MARRY

In I Timothy 3:1-5, the Apostle Paul gives Timothy the Lord's instructions on the qualifications of bishops and deacons. The Bible says:

> *This is a true saying, If a man desire the office of a bishop, he desireth a good work. A bishop then must be blameless, <u>the husband of one wife</u>, vigilant, sober, of good behaviour, given to hospitality, apt to teach; Not given to wine, no striker, not greedy of filthy lucre; but patient, not a brawler, not covetous; One that ruleth well his own house, having his children in subjection with all gravity; (For if a man know not how to rule his own house, how shall he take care of the church of God?)*

How Has the Lord's Early Church Been Changed? 51

The footnote in the 1966 Confraternity edition of *The Holy Bible* analyzes the word the Apostle Paul uses for "bishop." It acknowledges correctly that for Catholics "probably priests are here included under the term bishops." A further footnote to this passage explains that...

> ...*priestly celibacy as a law is of later ecclesiastical institution.*

In other words, this footnote in a Catholic Bible acknowledges that forbidding priests to marry was a change made as Church practices *evolved*. The ban became one of the *traditions* of the church.

Forbidding priests and bishops to marry was imposed or confirmed by a Church Council in the 11th Century. The Bible warned against this when the Apostle Paul wrote in I Timothy 4:1-3:

> *Now the Spirit speaketh expressly, that in the latter times some shall depart from the faith, giving heed to seducing spirits, and doctrines of devils; Speaking lies in hypocrisy; having their conscience seared with a hot iron; <u>forbidding to marry</u>, and commanding to abstain from meats which God hath created to be received with thanksgiving of them which believe and know the truth.*

This is another of the conflicts between the Bible and the current practice of the Catholic church. This is another conflict with my friend's statement and belief. He said of the faith the Lord Jesus gave us:

> *He did not leave us a Faith which needed to evolve. It was always there, absolute and immutable.*

NO MEAT ON FRIDAYS FOR CATHOLICS

From the time I was a small child until I was in my early 20s, I was taught that all Catholics had to abstain from eating meat on Fridays. To eat meat on Friday was, by Church law, a mortal sin. Until confessed and forgiven by a priest, the mortal sin of eating meat on Friday would doom the Catholic to Hell.

Again, the I Timothy 4:1-3 passage says:

Now the Spirit speaketh expressly, that in the latter times some shall depart from the faith, giving heed to seducing spirits, and doctrines of devils....<u>commanding to abstain from meats which God hath created to be received with thanksgiving of them which believe and know the truth.</u>

The teaching of the Church, according to both my friend and the *Baltimore Catechism* quoted earlier, cannot change if it is the true Church founded by the Lord.

The ban on eating meat *evolved* to become a church *tradition*. It was made a "mortal" sin [by papal edict of Pope Nicholas (A.D. 858-867) in the Dark Ages]. Recently, it *evolved* further. The ban on eating meat was abolished through a decision of Pope John Paul's Vatican II in the early 1960s. (A cynic might ask: "The Church taught for centuries that Catholics went to Hell for the unconfessed mortal sin of eating meat on Friday. Were they freed from Hell when the Pope at Vatican II changed what had been Church *law* for a thousand years?")

This ban on eating meat on Fridays, along with priestly celibacy, are among other conflicts between the teaching of the Word of God and the practice of the Catholic church.

Some of these conflicts might appear to be minor. However, none of God's instructions and commandments are to be taken lightly. They are conflicts between what the Bible teaches and commands— and the traditions introduced by the Roman church down through the centuries. One or the other has to be wrong — <u>truth cannot conflict with truth</u>.

HOW ARE SINS TO BE FORGIVEN?

As we have seen, some teachings of the Catholic Church conflict with the Word of God. Changing *traditions* sometimes are in conflict with previous traditions. The Catholic Church currently teaches, for example, that forgiveness is granted when sin is confessed to a priest. The practice is based on John 20:23. In a resurrection appearance, the Lord Jesus told the apostles:

> *Whose soever sins you remit, they are remitted unto them; and whose soever sins ye retain, they are retained.*

For the Apostles or priests to grant such forgiveness, the Church has taught that it is necessary to know specifically what the sins are. For this reason, the Church for years required audible confession to the priest.

However, there is no record in the New Testament that the apostles or anyone followed or taught such a practice.

How then were sins forgiven? In preaching to the Gentiles in the house of Cornelius, Peter told how sins were to be forgiven in Acts 10:42-43. He said that the Lord Jesus...

> *...commanded us to preach unto the people, and to testify that it is he which was ordained of God to be the Judge of quick and dead. To him give all the prophets witness, that through his name whosoever believeth in him shall receive remission of sins.*

The Apostles (and those who followed them) were to preach the Gospel. Those who believed, Acts 10:43 promises, would "receive remission of sins."

Once a person is saved, on-going sins which break fellowship with God are confessed directly to Him. The Apostle John in I John 1:9 omits confessing to an apostle or priest and promises:

> *If we confess our sins, he is faithful and just to forgive us our sins, and to cleanse us from all unrighteousness.*

The *1994 Catechism of the Catholic Church* acknowledges considerable on-going changes in Church teaching about forgiveness of sin. The Catechism on page 363 says:

> *Over the centuries the concrete form in which the Church has exercised this power received from the Lord [to forgive sins] has varied considerably....During the first centuries, serious sins were dealt with publicly....During*

> *the seventh century Irish missionaries, inspired by the Eastern monastic tradition, took to continental Europe the "private" practice of penance....From that time on the sacrament has been performed in secret between the penitent and priest....this is the form of penance that the Church has practiced down to our day.*

Since Vatican II, the 1994 Catechism indicates there were more changes. Perhaps because of the shortage of priests in some areas or pre-holiday pressures, instead of using the traditional one-on-one use of the confessional, the priest can grant forgiveness to an entire congregation. The Catechism says:

> *The sacrament of penance can also take place in the framework of a communal celebration....[and] a communal request for forgiveness....However, regardless of its manner of celebration the sacrament of Penance is always, by its very nature, a liturgical action. (Pg. 372)*

Age-old practices and traditions give way to what can become new traditions.

THE CRUCIAL MATTER OF SALVATION

The gravest conflict has to do with the most important question of all. It is the question the Philippian jailer asked the Apostle Paul in Acts Chapter 16. He came to Paul and Silas at midnight, crying:

Sirs, what must I do to be saved?

All other questions of life fade into insignificance when placed alongside those eight words. Finding the right answer — God's answer — to the question will determine whether or not we will be tormented in Hell for eternity — or if we will be rejoicing forever in the presence of Almighty God and His Son Jesus Christ.

Today, as down through the ages, people try to follow all sorts of man-made roads to Heaven. These man-made paths may pay some sort of lip service to what the Lord Jesus did on the Cross. But they then add involved programs of good works which are supposed to merit God's favor.

The way of *salvation* prescribed and taught by the Catholic Church becomes essentially a "works" program in the ears of the faithful. (People give mental assent to the message of faith, then seek assurance through the works in which they involve themselves.) The Catholic Catechism teaches an involved program of laws and works whereby people are saved— or keep the salvation they supposedly get— when sprinkled with water as an infant. The Baltimore Catechism (pgs. 168-169) teaches:

The laws of the Church are all directed to one great purpose— to bring men to eternal salvation...What are known as the six commandments of the church are in reality certain laws selected from the body of the Church's legislative enactments, stating the more urgent duties of the practical Catholic including attending Mass, observing certain days of fast and abstinence, supporting the Church financially, observing Church rules and regulations concerning marriage, and going to confession and communion at least once a year.

Breaking any of these church commandments willfully is a mortal sin. Catholics who observe them faithfully are regarded as practicing Catholics. Those who habitually neglect Mass and the laws of fast and abstinence are Catholics in name only. The church teaches that they are in grave danger of losing their souls. Anyone with one mortal sin cannot go to heaven, unless forgiven by a priest — or by God directly if a priest is not available.

PURGATORY

Even though sins are confessed and forgiven, Catholics must even so pay for their sins through works here on earth or by suffering in "purgatory." The 1994 Catechism, pages 268-69, says:

All who die in God's grace and friendship, but still imperfectly purified, are indeed assured of their eternal salvation, but after death they undergo purification [in purgatory], so as to achieve the holiness necessary to enter the joy of heaven.

However, the Bible in Hebrews 10:14 says of the Lord:

For by one offering <u>he hath perfected for ever</u> them that are sanctified.

When the Lord Jesus shed His blood on the Cross, Hebrews 10:14 teaches that He "perfected forever" those who trust Him for salvation. That being so, there is no need for a *purgatory* for further purification. *Purgatory* is not mentioned in the Book of Acts record of the early church or anywhere else in the New Testament.

Purgatory evolved through men's teaching over the centuries. It was declared to be binding Church dogma by the Council of Trent in the 1550s.

Even so, the Church devised a system whereby people can work themselves or loved ones out of their suffering in *purgatory*. The Catechism says:

The church has established a system of indulgences whereby the Catholic can "work out" in this life some of the punishment it teaches is due him in purgatory for his sins.

The *Catechism* in Question 435, page 248, defines an indulgence as...

...the remission granted by the Church of the temporal punishment due to sins already forgiven.

To gain these indulgences, the Catechism teaches that Catholics must "...perform the works required by the Church." The works may be applied to the Catholic's own account, or to the account of someone in purgatory.

What does the scripture say about making payments for our sins in purgatory before we can go to Heaven? In the 10th Chapter of Hebrews believers are given the assurance that Christ paid, *once for all,* for all their sins. The Scripture then gives further assurance. It repeats the Old Testament prophecy of the New Covenant which the Lord Jesus would bring in. Hebrews 10:14-16 says:

> *For by one offering, He [Christ] has perfected forever those who are sanctified. Thus also the Holy Spirit testifies unto us. For after having said, This is the covenant that I will make with them after those days, says the Lord: "I will put my laws upon their hearts, and upon their minds I will write them,"*

In verses 17-18, the Lord adds:

> *And their sins and their iniquities I will remember no more." Now where there is forgiveness of these, there is no longer any offering for sin.*

The Lord says here that He does not remember sins which have been forgiven. He promises that there is no more offering required for such sin. This the Scripture clearly teaches. How then can He keep tabs on how much suffering must be experienced in purgatory? Where does this leave the Catholic program of works to pay for — or avoid — temporal punishment in purgatory for sin?

The Catechism justifies its program of works and indulgences on the basis that they are "reasonable." It says:

> *Anyone who studies the Catholic doctrine of indulgence must admit that it is most reasonable...*

It doesn't matter whether a doctrine is reasonable. The question is, "Is it Biblical?" God's Word in Proverbs 14:12 warns about "reasonableness." It says:

> *Sometimes a way seems right to a man, but the end of it leads to death.*

Yet the Catholic Catechism says that the doctrine of indulgences...

> *...simply means that God in His mercy will accept the satisfactory works of some members of the Church for the benefit of others....God does the same when He accepts the satisfactions of His Divine Son and of the Saints in payment for the debt of temporal punishment due other*

members of the church. (Baltimore Catechism, pg. 252, para. 2)

To equate the infinite suffering of the sinless Savior on the Cross with the works of even the best of sinful men is incomprehensible. Men's works are never satisfactory in the eyes of God. That's why the Apostle Paul taught in Ephesians 2:8-9:

For by grace are ye saved through faith; and that not of yourselves, it is the gift of God: not of works, lest any man should boast.

If we can't earn salvation, what is our hope? That was the question the Philippian jailer was asking when he cried out to the Apostle Paul: "Sirs, what must I do to be saved?" In Acts 16:31, Paul answered:

Believe on the Lord Jesus Christ and thou shalt be saved, and thy household.

Note that the Apostle Paul didn't say, "Believe *about* the Lord Jesus Christ and thou shalt be saved." Instead, Paul said, "Believe *on* the Lord Jesus Christ..."

To be saved, the sinner must first recognize that Christ is Lord and therefore has the right to rule the individual's life.

Recognizing that he has violated God's rule over his life, the sinner must want a new life. He must also believe and trust that the blood Christ shed on the Cross totally satisfied the penalty God's justice demands for his prior refusal to have Christ as Lord. Romans 4:25 indicates that the resurrection of the Lord on the third day was the result of the Father accepting the sacrifice. The individual has been justified (made right with God) because the sin debt has been paid.

The Bible is settled. It cannot change. The Bible cannot change although it is sometimes ignored. Ultimately, the changes come to be regarded as Church "traditions."

That brings the next important question. Can Church *traditions* conflict with the Bible and still be true and valid? That question will be examined in the next chapter.

CHAPTER 8

SHOULD CHURCH TRADITIONS CONFLICT WITH THE BIBLE?

And He [the Lord Jesus] said unto them. Full well ye reject the commandment of God, that ye may keep your own tradition ... Making the word of God of none effect through your tradition, which ye have delivered; and many such like things do ye.
—*Mark 7:9, 13*

WHY DO CATHOLIC PRACTICES AND RITUALS appear to conflict directly with clear Biblical teachings?

There is an explanation. The Catholic Church teaches that in addition to the Bible, God also reveals His will through the *traditions* and practices which the church develops. It teaches that these evolving *traditions* and teachings of the Catholic Church are equal to the Bible in establishing truth and the means of salvation.

That is the teaching of the official 803-page, *1994 Catechism of the Catholic Church* produced under the direction of Joseph Cardinal Ratsinger, now Pope Benedict XVI. On page 26 this Catechism says that the [Catholic] Church...

> ...does not derive her certainty about all revealed truths from the holy Scriptures alone. Both Scripture and Tradition must be accepted and honored with equal sentiments of devotion and reverence.

Truth cannot conflict with truth. If truth is to be established, there cannot be any conflict or disagreement between Scripture and *Tradition*, if (as the Church teaches) Scripture and *Tradition* are of equal value.

Traditions which differed with the Bible led to the *Sola Scriptura* battle cry of the 16th Century Protestant Reformers. Those Latin words translate as "Only Scripture!" or "Scripture Alone!"

THE BIBLE AND TRADITION

The concept that *Tradition* and Scripture have equal value as sources of truth produces deep concern. The Lord Jesus warned us to beware of *Tradition* in religious life. In Mark 7:13, the Lord was addressing the Pharisees sect, the religious formalists of that day. The Pharisees put great emphasis on ceremony. They worked very hard through fasting, reciting of prayers, observing man-made rules, etc. to achieve righteousness. They sought righteousness through 600 rules and *traditions* which they added to what God said in the Old Testament.

The Pharisees hoped to become good enough for God through such rules and *traditions*. They considered themselves God's chosen priests on earth. Those who served in the temple sacrificed animals. They put such emphasis on their own rules and rituals that they lost sight of God's Word. They believed in God. They accepted the Scriptures. They continually referred to "Moses and the prophets" (The Old Testament scriptures). Yet because of their *traditions* they completely missed the real message of the Old Testament. As a result, they did not recognize Jesus as the promised Messiah when He came. In Mark 7:13, the Lord Jesus chastised them for...

> ...*making the Word of God of none effect through your tradition.*

In the Confraternity edition of the Catholic Bible Mark 7:13 reads, *"You make void the commandment of God by your tradition, which you have handed down..."* A few verses earlier, the Lord said to them, *"Well you do nullify the Commandment of God that you may keep your own tradition."* These words were spoken by the Lord to the Pharisees. The record was left to be a warning and to serve as a guide to us today— as all scripture should be. In that regard, Pius XII, in the *Encyclical on Reading the Sacred Scripture* quoted *II Timothy 3:16* which says:

> *All scripture is inspired by God and is useful for teaching, for reproving, for correcting, for instructing in justice [righteousness].*

In other words, scripture is the authority even today. The Apostle Paul issued a similar warning. In Colossians 2:8 he wrote:

> *Beware lest any man spoil you through philosophy and vain deceit, <u>after the tradition of men,</u> after the rudiments of the world, and not after Christ.*

The admonitions of Paul and the Lord do not outlaw *tradition* per se. However, the Lord makes it clear that there is a danger that men can make *tradition* supersede or replace the Word of God. The danger is to "make the Word of God of no effect" through *traditions*.

Jesus warned time and again, *"The scripture cannot be broken."* In other words, there cannot be two contradictory sources of "truth." Truth must agree with truth. Truth cannot be changed. The Lord Jesus Christ in John 14:6 said:

> *I am the way, the truth and the life. No man cometh unto the father, but by me.*

Hebrews 13:8 says...

> *Jesus Christ the same yesterday, and today, and forever.*

Like Jesus Christ, the Word of God, which is truth, never changes. Psalm 119:89 says:

Forever, O Lord, thy word is settled in Heaven.

The Apostle Paul also spelled out in a very definite way that the Gospel is unchangeable. Paul wrote to the churches in Galatia. The Christians there, having been saved through faith in Jesus Christ, started listening to some false teachers. The false teachers had come from Jerusalem where some of the Apostles were teaching. The false teachers told the

Galatian believers that it was fine to get saved by faith— but once they were saved that it was necessary to work to keep their salvation. New believers, the false teachers said, were instructed to go on to perfection by observing certain laws, fasts, ceremonies and *traditions*. To validate their teaching the false teachers reported (correctly) that even Peter (who the Catholic Church teaches was the first Pope) was practicing some of these things. Paul, inspired by the Holy Spirit, denied this. In Galatians 1:8-9 Paul replied with this warning:

But even if we or an angel from Heaven should preach to you other than that which we have preached to you, let him be anathema [cursed]! As we have said before, so now I say again: if anyone preach a gospel to you other than that which you have received, let him be anathema!

That is strong language. However, the point is made: the doctrine taught in the Word of God cannot be changed. It cannot be changed by one of the Apostles personally selected by the Lord— or even by an angel from Heaven.

Even in New Testament times the Apostles themselves were subjected to having their teaching checked against the Old Testament scriptures. When Paul and Silas were in Thessalonica (Acts 17:1-9) the Jews stirred up violent opposition against them. To protect them, the Thessalonican believers sent Paul and Silas away to Berea. There they preached the Word in the Berean synagogue. Acts 17:11 then tells us...

These [the Bereans] were more noble than those in Thessalonica, in that they received the word with all readiness of mind, and searched the scriptures daily, whether those things were so.

The Holy Spirit had Luke, the human author of the Book of Acts, commend the Bereans. They checked everything, (even what an Apostle said) against the scripture. Today, we are commanded in I Thessalonians 5:21:

Prove all things, hold fast that which is good.

The Bible— God's Word— is the only unchanging, inerrant standard by which to test and prove "all things."

When I was a boy, the Catholic Church taught us that the Church alone was competent to interpret and apply scripture correctly. For that reason, few Catholics did much Bible reading. The current *Catechism*, on page 20, teaches, even today, that the Catholic Church is the only authoritative interpreter of Scripture. It says:

The task of interpreting the Word of God authentically has been entrusted solely to the Magisterium of the Church, to the Pope and to the bishops in communion with him.

However, the Bible passage quoted from Acts 17:11 shows that God commended the individuals in Berea as being "more noble" than those in Thessalonica. The Bereans studied the scriptures daily. They checked to see for themselves whether the teaching, even of an Apostle, was true and in agreement with God's Word.

The Apostle John also contradicted the concept that only the church and its leaders are qualified to give the correct understanding of God's Word. In I John 2:25-27 John wrote to believers, saying:

And this is the promise that he hath promised us, even eternal life. These things have I written unto you concerning them that seduce you. But the anointing which ye have received of him [the Holy Spirit] abideth in you, and ye need not that any man teach you: but as the same anointing teacheth you of all things, and is truth, and is no lie, and even as it hath taught you, ye shall abide in him.

This was another cry of the 16th Century Reformers, who believed and taught that the Holy Spirit could give individual believers understanding of the Word of God. By that time the Bible had been translated into the languages of various peoples everywhere. The invention of the printing press made widespread distribution of the Bible available to people. Widespread distribution of the Bible in the language of the people produced what is called today the *Protestant Reformation*. People who read and studied the scriptures found definite conflicts between what the Bible said and the teaching and practice of the Roman Church.

The Holy Spirit comes into the hearts of those who trust Christ to be their personal Savior (Galatians 4:6). The Holy Spirit then teaches the believer. When opening the Bible, we should pray the prayer in Psalm 119:18:

Open thou mine eyes that I may behold wondrous things out of thy law.

The Bible is a spiritual book. It should be spiritually understood. Before I was born again I had great difficulty understanding anything but the simplest passages. Why? I Corinthians 2:14 says:

But the natural man [unsaved] receiveth not the things of the Spirit of God for they are foolishness unto him; neither can he know them because they are spiritually discerned.

The first indication that I was saved was that the Bible suddenly started making sense. When I believed, the Holy Spirit came into my heart. The Bible became a "new" book. God's Spirit started teaching me the Bible's meaning. Before that I was a "natural" man. I could not perceive the things of the Spirit— which the Bible is.

The chapters which follow will explore other Catholic traditions and teachings which conflict with the Word of God.

CHAPTER 9

BAPTISM AND THE BIBLE: WHY, WHO, WHEN AND HOW?

And Jesus came and spoke unto them saying ... Go ye therefore and teach all nations, baptizing them in the name of the Father, and of the Son, and of the Holy Ghost: Teaching them to observe all things whatsoever I have commanded you ...
— *Matthew 28:18-20*

MY OWN STUDY OF THE BIBLE resolved the struggle I was having over whether my baptism as an infant was a valid Christian baptism. Did I really need to be baptized again? This is a very important issue to get resolved. The Lord's command to be baptized is clear. But how, when and why it is to be done is vitally important.

The division and dissension among churches and Christians over baptism show that the proper time, method and reason for baptism must be important. Otherwise Satan wouldn't spend so much time trying to confuse and divide Christians over the issue.

The question is: "Have you been scripturally baptized?" The answer should not be based on church teaching or what an individual feels is right. To determine whether a person has been scripturally baptized, it is necessary to know what the Bible teaches about (1) who should be baptized, (2) what baptism means or pictures and (3) the correct method of baptism.

WHO SHOULD BE BAPTIZED?

The Bible teaches clearly and specifically that only believers are to be baptized. The Book of Acts records events which show how the early church did things. Acts 8:34-39 describes how God sent Philip, an evangelist, to help an Ethiopian eunuch come to faith. The eunuch was in his chariot, returning home to Ethiopia. History indicates that he was Secretary of the Treasury of Ethiopia. He had been to Jerusalem to investigate the religion of the Jews. He obtained a copy of their scriptures. Today, we know the Jewish scriptures as our *Old Testament.* As the eunuch rode in his chariot, he was studying the Old Testament prophecy of the coming Messiah in Isaiah Chapter 53. The twelve verses in that chapter were written 700 years before Christ. Being prophecy, they detail how and why the Messiah was to come and what He would do through His death, burial and resurrection. For example, Isaiah 53:6 says words which clearly apply to Christ and to us:

All we like sheep have gone astray; we have turned every one to his own way; and the Lord hath laid on him the iniquity of us all.

The eunuch continued reading Isaiah 53 as he rode. Acts 8:30-33 which records the incident then says:

And Philip [the evangelist] ran thither to him, and heard him read the prophet Esaias, and said, Understandest thou what thou readest? And he said, How can I, except some man should guide me? And he desired Philip that he would come up and sit with him.

The Ethiopian was reading in Isaiah 53 of the coming Messiah, His rejection by men, His death and burial. The eunuch asked Philip...

I pray thee, of whom speaketh the prophet this? of himself, or of some other man? Then Philip opened his mouth, and began at the same scripture, and preached unto him Jesus.

The scripture then says:

And as they went on their way, they came unto a certain water: and the eunuch said, See, here is water; what doth hinder me to be baptized?

While in Jerusalem, the eunuch apparently had been exposed to the teaching of the newly forming Christian church concerning baptism. The eunuch asked Philip that vitally important question, "What doth hinder me to be baptized?"

In Acts 8:37, Philip answered, placing this condition on baptizing the Ethiopian eunuch:

> *And Philip said, If thou believest with all thine heart, thou mayest. And he answered and said, I believe that Jesus Christ is the Son of God.*

Upon his profession of faith in Jesus Christ, the scripture says:

> *And he commanded the chariot to stand still: and they went down both into the water, both Philip and the eunuch; and he baptized him. And when they were come up out of the water, the Spirit of the Lord caught away Philip, that the eunuch saw him no more: and he went on his way rejoicing.*

Acts 8:37 makes faith in Jesus Christ the condition for baptism. As important as the answer in Acts 8:37 is, the verse has been removed, questioned or denied in some widely distributed *recent* translations of the Bible. With Acts 8:37 missing or questioned, these widely promoted recent translations may find more acceptance in churches and denominations which do not require belief before baptism. They sprinkle infants (and others).

Personal faith in the death, burial and resurrection of Christ is the Bible prerequisite for baptism. Every person baptized in the Book of Acts was shown to have heard and believed the Word of God before being baptized. The Book of Acts is our record of how the early church did things. There are seven such accounts in the Book of Acts on how the early church practiced baptism in addition to the one already described. They are found in Acts 2:41; 8:12-13; 9:17-18; 16:14-15; 16:30-33; 18:8; and 19:4-5. The question of who should be baptized is important enough that every one of the passages has been listed here. Each of these passages show that people heard the word and believed before they were baptized. The passages are:

ACTS 2:41: Then they that gladly received his word were baptized: and the same day there were added unto them about three thousand souls.

ACTS 8:12-13: But when they believed Philip preaching the things concerning the kingdom of God, and the name of Jesus Christ, they were baptized, both men and women. Then Simon himself believed also: and when he was baptized, he continued with Philip, and wondered, beholding the miracles and signs which were done.

ACTS 9:17-18: Brother Saul, the Lord, even Jesus, that appeared unto thee in the way as thou camest, hath sent me, that thou mightest receive thy sight, and be filled with the Holy Ghost. And immediately there fell from his eyes as it had been scales: and he received sight forthwith, and arose, and was baptized.

ACTS 16:14-15: And a certain woman named Lydia, a seller of purple, of the city of Thyatira, which worshipped God, heard us: whose heart the Lord opened, that she attended unto the things which were spoken of Paul. And when she was baptized, and her household, she besought us, saying, If ye have judged me to be faithful to the Lord, come into my house, and abide there...

ACTS 16:30-33: [The jailer] said: Sirs, what must I do to be saved? And they said, Believe on the Lord Jesus Christ, and thou shalt be saved, and thy house. And they spake unto him the word of the Lord, and to all that were in his house. And he took them the same hour of the night, and washed their stripes; and was baptized, he and all his, straightway.

ACTS 18:8: And Crispus, the chief ruler of the synagogue, believed on the Lord with all his house; and many of the Corinthians hearing believed, and were baptized.

> *ACTS 19:4-5: Then said Paul, John verily baptized with the baptism of repentance, saying unto the people, that they should believe on him which should come after him, that is, on Christ Jesus. When they heard this, they were baptized in the name of the Lord Jesus.*

Note carefully that in every instance those who were baptized heard the Word of God and believed before they were baptized. Two passages do indicate that the individual's family was baptized also. That they were not infants but older children is shown because in each instance the passage indicates that they were all first given the Word of God.

WHAT DOES BAPTISM PICTURE?

Not only did Jesus Christ die on the cross for our personal sins, but the Bible also teaches that our old life also died with Him. *Romans 6:6-7* says:

> *Knowing this, that our old man [the original sinful life we got from Adam] is crucified with him, that the body of sin might be destroyed, that henceforth we should not serve [be a slave to] sin. For he that is dead is freed from sin.*

The Epistle to the churches of Galatia has the same message. *Galatians 2:20* presents the testimony of those whose old sinful life died with Christ on the cross, who were buried with Him and who were resurrected to a new life in Him. The Apostle Paul wrote:

> *I am crucified with Christ: nevertheless I live; yet not I, but Christ liveth in me: and the life which I now live in the flesh I live by the faith of the Son of God, who loved me, and gave himself for me.*

When we are baptized, we are testifying, "I believe that Christ died for my sins, was buried and then raised again the third day. When He died, my old life died with Him. When I believed I was raised to new life in Christ." This becomes real in our lives through faith when we believe.

CORRECT METHOD OF BAPTISM

When we are immersed [buried] in water, we are testifying and picturing that our old life ended and that we were raised to a new life in Christ when we believed.

That the early church's baptismal practice was as set forth above was confirmed in an April 1971 Easter message by Terrance Cardinal Cooke, Archbishop of New York. In a special April 10-11, 1971, Easter section of the *St. Louis Globe Democrat*, Cardinal Cooke said:

> *In the earliest centuries of Christianity, the baptismal font was a pool. The person who was to be united with Christ in Baptism went down into the pool, was baptized and then arose up out of the pool. And the going into and coming out of the pool symbolized union with Christ in the tomb — dying with Christ and rising with Him to a new life. And that symbolism of baptism we should remember particularly in these [Easter] days.*

Cardinal Cooke acknowledges that baptism in the earliest days of Christianity was different. Why, then, has the Catholic Church changed the time, method and meaning of baptism?

HAVE YOU BEEN BAPTIZED SCRIPTURALLY?

In the Book of Acts all who were baptized in the early church, were believers. They had placed their trust in Christ — that His death, burial and resurrection was for them personally. They were saved.

Can you look back to when you believed not just *about* Christ, but that He died for *you personally*? Can you look back to when your old life ended and you became a new creation in and through Jesus Christ?

Have you been immersed in water since you were saved as a testimony that you believe that Christ died for you, was buried and arose again from the dead?

Chapter 10

WHY DO FEW CHURCHES PREACH "YE MUST BE BORN AGAIN"?

Jesus answered [Nicodemus] and said unto him, Verily, Verily, I say unto thee. Except a man be born again, he cannot see [nor enter] the Kingdom of God ... Marvel not that I said unto thee, Ye must be born again.
— *John 3:3, 5, 7*

IN 1965 I STARTED MY SEARCH TO FIND THE CHURCH OF GOD'S CHOICE. The search started after I believed that the Lord Jesus had died, not just for the sins of the world, but for *me*. When I, a sinner, knew that I needed a new life, I trusted that He died for *me* and was raised again. By faith, I was born into God's family. I became a new person. The Bible came alive to me and was like a new book. I talked to the Lord rather than just saying prayers. As I started to enjoy my new life in Christ, I started to wonder and ask...

When I was growing up as a Catholic why had I never heard that Jesus said, "Ye must be born again?"

The teaching that "Ye must be born again" largely disappeared when the "evolving" Catholic system changed the time, method and meaning of baptism. As the previous chapter shows, the Bible records that every person baptized in the early Church believed *first*. However, history indicates that some churches started baptizing infants as early as the Third Century. Infant baptism became a law in some places by about A.D. 400 as Church and State were merged.

The most recent 803-page *Catechism of the Catholic Church* was published in 1994. That Catechism carries the *Imprimi Potest* (official approval) of Joseph Cardinal Ratzinger.

Ratzinger is now Pope Benedict XVI. On page 322-23, the Catechism tells what happens when an infant is baptized. It says:

> *Baptism not only purifies from all sins, but also makes the neophyte "a new creature," an adopted son of God, who has become "a partaker of the divine nature"....From the baptismal fonts is <u>born</u> the one People of God of the New Covenant....<u>Reborn</u> as sons of God, [the baptized] must profess before men the faith they have received from God through the Church. (Emphasis added.)*

The Gospel of St. John teaches a very different way of being born into God's family. John 1:1-10 identifies the Lord Jesus as God, the Creator and Messiah. In verses 11-13, the Scripture tells how individuals are born into God's family. The Bible says of Jesus:

> *He came unto his own, and his own received him not. But as many as received him, to them gave he power to become the sons of God, <u>even to them that believe on his name:</u> Which were born, not of blood, nor of the will of the flesh, nor of the will of man, but of God. (Emphasis added.)*

We are born into God's family when we believe that Jesus Christ died for our personal sins and that He was buried and then raised from the dead three days later. The Lord Jesus becomes the new life of those who want a new life and receive Him to be Lord and Savior.

The change from believers' baptism to infant baptism has affected the teaching and practice of the Roman Catholic Church. It has also affected the practice and theology of those Protestant churches which came out of the Roman church at the time of the Reformation. Such churches brought some *traditions* and practices of Catholicism, including infant baptism, with them.

About 1600 years ago certain portions of the Gospels and Epistles were selected and designated to be read each Sunday in the Churches. These churches were then in the process of becoming part of what is now the Roman system. Many churches did not have complete Bibles. For them, selected portions of the Gospels and Epistles were copied and read in services. Those selected readings are being used today in Catholic and some non-catholic churches.

These readings came largely from those parts of the scriptures written to instruct saved people on how to live. When the schedules of readings were developed by the churches in the evolving Roman system, such churches believed that people in their congregations were already born again. They were thought to have been born again when they were sprinkled with water as infants or upon joining the church later in life.

Because the hearers were considered to be saved already by their baptism, it was not necessary to have salvation passages read to them regularly. Instead the selected readings emphasized the later chapters of the writings of Paul, Peter, James and John which teach saved, regenerated people how to live.

When I started my study as a newly saved Christian many years ago, I got the 1967 *Catholic Sunday Missal*. Serious Catholics carry the missal to Mass. It contains Mass prayers and responses and the weekly Gospel and Epistle readings. I read the 110 (about) scheduled gospels and epistles for the year. They were for the most part readings which had been selected about 1600 years before. Of these, I found less than ten which contained the word "saved" as it applies to forgiveness and everlasting life. *Saved* appears in various forms over 100 times in the Gospels and Epistles. But it was largely missing in the Catholic Missal readings.

The "censoring" stems logically from the changed theology which came with the *evolving* meaning and mode of baptism. If all church members were "saved" when they were sprinkled with water as infants, they didn't need to be challenged regularly with passages of scripture which taught the need to be "saved." From that point on they just had to live good enough so as not to lose the salvation they supposedly received when they were sprinkled with water as infants.

A variety of churches retained infant baptism when they broke with Catholicism in the Reformation. Some, like Lutherans and Anglicans (Episcopalians) believe that infant baptism saves. Methodist parents who have their children baptized as infants are promising to train them up in the Church. Presbyterians and others in the Reformed tradition baptize infants but relate it to the Old Testament practice of circumcision.

Infant baptism affects the teaching, ritual and preaching in a church. People hear how they should live. Rarely are they brought face-to-face with their need for the new birth and new nature. But individuals can live the Christian life only through the new birth. The more orthodox among those who baptize infants also emphasize in various ways and degrees that personal faith in Jesus Christ and the new birth must follow.

John Wesley came to personal faith in Christ after 13 years of ministry in the Episcopal Church. He started to preach that even if you have been baptized as an infant, "Jesus says: Ye must be born again." Wesley added, "That's true, even if you are an Anglican rector or bishop."

In John 3:3, the Lord Jesus told a very religious man, "Verily, Verily, I say unto thee. Except a man be born again, He cannot see [nor enter] the Kingdom of God.

Ideas have consequences. Wrong ideas have tragic consequences, especially if the wrong ideas ignore the Bible and the Bible way of doing things.

CHAPTER 11

THE CATHOLIC MASS

Prove [test] all things; hold fast that which is good .... All scripture is given by inspiration of God, and is profitable for doctrine, for reproof, for correction, for instruction in righteousness. That the man of God may be perfect, thoroughly furnished unto all good works.
— *1 Thessalonians 5:21, II Timothy 3:16-17*

THE MASS IS THE CENTER OF CATHOLIC EXPERIENCE AND PRACTICE. What Catholics call *Transubstantiation* is at the heart of Church teaching about the Mass.

Transubstantiation is the belief that when, at Mass, the priest repeats the Last Supper words of the Lord, *"This is My Body— This is My Blood,"* the bread and wine for communion are miraculously transformed into the actual body and blood of Christ. This doctrine was first made official in the Fourth Catholic Council of the Lateran in 1215 and was reaffirmed in the 1500s by the Council of Trent.

Both the traditional *Baltimore Catechism* and the newer *1994 Catechism of the Catholic Church* spell out the benefits from the Mass. *Transubstantiation* is the basis for each. The three principal benefits are:

> *During Mass, the Catechism teaches that through the words of the priest, the Lord Jesus Christ becomes present in the transformed bread and wine to be re-sacrificed in an unbloody manner. The re-sacrificed Christ is then offered to God by the priest to pay for the on-going sins of the people.*

In the communion part of the Mass, Catholics are taught by both Catechisms that they receive spiritual nourishment and strength by eating and drinking the actual body and blood of Christ.

During the Mass, Catholics are taught that the Lord Jesus Christ, who is present in the bread and wine of the communion elements through transubstantiation, is to be worshiped and adored by those present.

After Mass, the transformed bread and wine not distributed in communion is stored in a tabernacle in the church to be visited, worshipped, adored and prayed to by the faithful who visit the church.

When Martin Luther, a Catholic priest, broke with Rome over selling indulgences, Luther also rejected *transubstantiation*. Instead, Luther, and Lutherans today, teach *consubstantiation*. *Consubstantiation* is the teaching that when the communicant receives the bread and wine at communion it becomes the body and blood of Christ through the individual's personal faith. Most other non-Catholic churches teach that the bread and fruit of the vine are received at communion simply in remembrance of what He did through His death, burial and resurrection.

What the Catholic Catechisms teach about the Mass and the doctrine of Transubstantiation and benefits for each will be examined Biblically in the chapters that follow.

CHAPTER 12

CAN CHRIST BE RE-SACRIFICED DAILY IN CATHOLIC CHURCHES?

So Christ was <u>once</u> offered to bear the sins of many....we are sanctified through the offering of the body of Jesus Christ <u>once and for all</u>...after he had offered <u>one</u> sacrifice for sins forever, sat down on the right hand of God...for by ONE OFFERING he hath perfected forever them that are sanctified.
— Hebrews 9:28, 10:10, 10:12, 10:14

A SERIOUS CONFLICT EXISTS between Bible teaching and the Catholic Catechism. The Catechism says that Christ is re-sacrificed for sin at Mass on Catholic altars.

When I started my search for God's church over forty years ago, I obtained *The Catholic Baltimore Catechism*. That Catechism teaches that Jesus Christ is bodily present in the Mass. During Mass, the bread and wine used in communion are transformed into the actual body and blood of Christ through the words of the priest. According to the Catholic Catechism, Jesus is there at every Mass to be re-sacrificed again and again by the priests. The Church teaches that the sacrifice of Christ on Calvary's Cross is renewed and repeated at every Mass.

This re-sacrificing of Christ, in what the Church calls an unbloody manner, is to pay for on-going sins of mankind committed since Calvary. However, the Bible teaches that on the Cross, the Lord Jesus completed the sacrificial work He came to do and said, "It is finished!" That was the final sacrifice.

The Baltimore Catechism, Lesson 27, pages 207-211 says that the Mass is not just a memorial service like the communion services in non-Catholic churches. Instead, the Mass is an actual re-sacrifice of Christ. The Catechism in Questions 359, 360, 361, and 362 teaches:

> *The principal priest in every Mass is Jesus Christ, Who offers to His Heavenly Father, through the ministry of His ordained priest, His Body and Blood which were sacrificed on the Cross. The Mass is the same sacrifice as the sacrifice of the Cross.*

The Church teaches that the Mass is the same sacrifice as the sacrifice of the Cross. In the Mass the victim, Jesus Christ, is the same, and the principal priest is the same, Jesus Christ. In the Mass Christ functions through His ordained human priest. Catechism Questions 361-2 explain...

> *...the Mass is offered...to satisfy the justice of God for the [on-going] sins committed against Him.*

> *On the cross Christ was offered in a bloody manner; On the cross Christ alone offered Himself directly; in the Mass He offers Himself through the priest.*

For many centuries, all over the world, Catholic priests have daily conducted Masses in which the Church teaches that the Lord Jesus is re-sacrificed.

The authoritative Catholic Council of Trent in the mid-1500s pronounced and published the Canons on the Sacrifice of the Mass. In its series of pronouncements, the Council proclaimed an *ANATHAMA* (a curse) on those who would deny that the Mass is a re-sacrificing of Jesus Christ by priests on Catholic altars

This teaching is in direct conflict with the Bible which again and again teaches that Christ died "once for all."

THE BIBLE AND THE MASS

Specifically, how does the Bible conflict with what the Catholic Church calls the Sacrifice of the Mass? The principal teachings about the priesthood of Jesus Christ and of His offering of Himself <u>once for all</u> as a sacrifice for our sins are found primarily in the Epistle to the Hebrews.

Hebrews was written about A.D. 65. It was written not to a particular church, as most other Epistles were, but to Jewish Christians. It was written both to those who were actual saved believers and also to those who just professed to believe. People in both groups were wavering — trying to keep feet in both camps. Many tried to continue in both the Old Jewish system and also in the New Testament churches.

They were wavering because Jewish Christians were being subjected to great persecution. By accepting Christ, they faced pressure and persecution from their families, their business associates, their communities and the Jewish religious leaders. Some went back to the temple and were again offering animal sacrifices for their sins. They weren't fully trusting that the shed blood of the Lord Jesus Christ was the complete payment for their sins.

The two-fold purpose of the book of Hebrews was (1) to reassure the actual Jewish Christians and (2) to bring the professing ones to full faith in the Lord Jesus. The theme of the book of Hebrews is that "Jesus Christ is better." Hebrews shows that Christ is better than the angels, better than Moses, better than the old Levitical priesthood. The epistle teaches that Christ's sacrifice is better than the old sacrifices under the Law, and that His New Covenant is superior to the Old.

The book of Hebrews was written to Hebrew believers in the same way that Ephesians was written to the church at Ephesus, Galatians to the churches in Galatia, etc. However, each of those Epistles, including Hebrews, are relevant for us today. The Apostle Paul, under the inspiration of the Holy Ghost in II Timothy 3:16, explained:

> <u>All</u> *scripture is given by inspiration of God and* <u>is</u> *profitable for doctrine, for reproof, for correction, for instruction in righteousness. (Emphasis added.)*

All scripture, rightly applied, has a message for us today. What does the message about Christ and His priesthood (as described in Hebrews) tell us today? Does it have any application or relevance to the teaching of the Catholic Church and its Catechism? The Church and its Catechism both teach that Christ is re-sacrificed daily in every Mass "to satisfy the justice of God for the sin committed against Him" (Q. 361-362, pg. 209). If the Lord Jesus needs to be re-crucified daily, His sacrificial work on the Cross was not actually completed when He cried out, "It is finished:" bowed his head, and gave up the ghost. (John 19:30)

The book of Hebrews compares the priesthood of Jesus Christ with the Levitical priesthood of the Old Testament. Hebrews 7:27 says of the Lord Jesus...

> *...who needeth not daily, as those high priests, to offer up sacrifice, first for his own sins, and then for the people's: for this he did <u>once</u>, when he offered up himself.*

The conflict with the Catechism is also shown in the 1946 Catholic Confraternity Edition of the Bible. It translates Hebrews 7:27 in the same way the King James Version does:

> *He [Christ] does not need to offer sacrifices daily [as the Old Testament priests did] first for his own sins, and then for the sins of the people; for this he did <u>once for all</u> in offering up Himself.*

Hebrews 9:26-28 in the same Catholic version adds:

> *But now, <u>once for all</u>, at the end of the ages, He has appeared for the destruction of sin by sacrifice of Himself. And just as it is appointed unto man to die once, after this comes the judgments, <u>so also was Christ offered once</u> to take away the sins of many.*

Most of the newer versions of the Bible have the same *once for all* message. Hebrews 10:11, 12 and 14 contrasts the sacrifice Christ offered with those of Old Testament priests. The contrast is emphasized in Hebrew 10:11-12 when speaking of the Old Testament priests, the King James Version says:

> *And every priest indeed standeth daily ministering, and often offering the same sacrifices, which can never take*

away sins; but Jesus <u>having offered one sacrifice for sins,</u>has taken His seat forever at the right hand of God... <u>For by one offering</u> He has perfected forever those who are sanctified.

In a strict sense, the writer of Hebrews, in this passage, is looking back at the sacrifices of the Old Testament Levitical priesthood. However, on the basis of II Timothy 3:16, we can apply the principle today. The writer of Hebrews, inspired by the Holy Spirit, admonishes wavering Jewish Christians. They were told that they did not need to go back to the Jewish temple to offer animal sacrifices for their sins because Christ had died for them *once for all*.

The writer of Hebrews did not point these wavering believers to the Mass or any other form of continual, on-going sacrifice of Christ for sin. The writer of Hebrews doesn't say, "Come to the Lord's Supper at Mass; and have the merits of Christ's sacrifice applied to you. If you do, you won't have to go to the temple and sacrifice animals."

If the Catholic Mass is a continuing sacrifice of Christ's Body and Blood to satisfy God's justice for sins against Him, wouldn't wavering Jewish Christians have been directed to it? This would have been a powerful argument. <u>But this is not done.</u> Instead, repeatedly, the Bible says that Christ was offered <u>once for all</u>. Reread Hebrews 7:27, 9:26-28, 10:11-14.

The Bible's repeated insistence that Christ was offered <u>once for all</u> is in complete conflict with what the Catholic Catechism teaches about Christ being re-sacrificed for sin in the Mass. His sacrificial work of suffering was complete. <u>He did not need to die again.</u>

The Apostle Paul confirms that there is no need for Christ to be re-sacrificed daily. In Romans 6:9-10, Paul wrote:

Knowing that <u>Christ being raised from the dead dieth no more</u>; death hath no more dominion over Him. For in that He died, <u>He died unto sin once</u>; in that He liveth, He liveth unto God.

The Apostle John in the Book of Revelation quotes the Lord Jesus Himself as saying that He was alive for evermore. In Revelation 1:18, the Lord Jesus told John:

I am he that liveth, and was dead; and, <u>behold, I am alive for evermore</u>...

So, the Apostle Paul's Epistle to the Church at Rome, the Book of Hebrews and the Book of Revelation all show that the Catholic Catechism's teaching about the Mass is in conflict with the Bible. Christ doesn't need to be re-sacrificed daily on Catholic altars for sin. He died on the *once for all* and is alive for evermore.

Each reader needs to answer personally the question. "Do I know for sure and am I trusting *fully* that when the Lord Jesus died on the Cross, He died for *all of my* personal sins?"

CHAPTER 13

DOES TAKING COMMUNION FEED THE SOUL?

And when the tempter [Satan] came to him, he said, If thou be the Son of God, command that these stones be made bread. But he [Jesus] answered and said, It is written, Man shall not live by bread alone, but by every word that proceedeth out of the mouth of God.
— *Matthew 4:3-4*

TRANSUBSTANTIATION is the Catholic teaching that those those who take the bread and wine at communion in the Mass are actually partaking of the body and blood of the Lord Jesus. The Catholic teaching is that the bread and wine are actually changed into the body and blood of the Lord when the priest repeats the Lord's words from the Last Supper at Mass.

A sub-chapter in the *1994 Catechism of the Catholic Church* titled, "The Fruits of Holy Communion," spells out the benefits Catholics receive from taking communion at Mass. This Catechism, prepared under the supervision of Joseph Cardinal Ratzinger (now Pope Benedict XVI), says on page 351:

> *What material food produces in our bodily life, Holy Communion wonderfully achieves in our spiritual life. Communion with the flesh of the risen Christ, a flesh "given life through the Holy Spirit," preserves, increases, and renews the life of grace received at Baptism. This growth in Christian life needs the nourishment of Eucharistic Communion, the bread for our pilgrimage until the moment of death.*

The Catechism quotes John 6:53 as the basis for requiring Catholics to partake at communion of what they believe to be the Lord's actual body and blood. That verse says:

> *Then Jesus said unto them, Verily, verily, I say unto you, Except ye eat the flesh of the Son of man, and drink his blood, ye have no life in you.*

The Lord made this statement several years before He actually instituted the Lord's Supper. It is the basis for the Church claiming that taking communion at Mass bestows spiritual nourishment and strength derived from the actual body and blood of the Lord Jesus. This interpretation was made an official doctrine of the Catholic Church in the mid-1500s at the Council of Trent.

Teaching that partaking of communion at Mass provides spiritual nourishment for the soul is in conflict with the teaching of both the Lord Jesus and the Apostle Peter.

IS COMMUNION FOOD FOR THE SOUL?

In Matthew 4:3, the Lord, before starting His public ministry, had been fasting for forty days and nights. Then, in the first of three temptations, the Lord Jesus, Who was hungry, was challenged by Satan to turn stones into bread.

> *But he [Jesus] answered and said, It is written, Man shall not live by bread alone, <u>but by every word that proceedeth out of the mouth of God.</u>*

It is the Word of God, Jesus said, through which we receive nourishment to live and grow spiritually.

The Apostle Peter, in I Peter 2:2, taught the same view. Peter said that nourishment for the soul and true spiritual growth comes from careful study and feeding on God's Word, the Bible. In I Peter 2:2, Peter wrote to newly born-again believers, saying:

> *As newborn babes, desire the sincere milk of the word, that ye may grow thereby.*

That is why, in the early churches, services emphasized the preaching and teaching of the Word of God rather than rituals. After the teaching and preaching, services concluded, *catechumens* (those who were not yet saved and baptized) were dismissed so believers could have the Lord's Supper (communion).

Origen was one of the most prominent theologians among the Church Fathers in the third century. Early in Church history, he, like Peter and the Lord, taught a different view from current catechisms. Origen worked in Alexandria and Caesarea. He was regarded as the premier theologian between the Apostle Paul and St. Augustine. He became controversial with later church leaders. Origen placed more emphasis on the Word of God and the spiritual concepts behind the developing sacramental rituals of the Church than on the rituals themselves. The 1955 book, *Origen,* by the French Catholic author Jean Danielou, said that Origen was...

> ...interested in the visible signs of worship only in so far as they were signs of spiritual things....He emphasized preaching rather than the liturgy (pg. 52).

His biographer said that one of the concepts which made Origen controversial was the impression that...

> ...he somewhat underrates the Eucharist when compared with the spiritual eating of the Word in Scripture. "Eating of the Word" in scripture, Origen taught, is a sacrament or basis for receiving grace (pg. 65).

In other words, Origen believed and taught that grace for salvation and for living life is received by faith. Grace for salvation and spiritual growth, he taught, comes as God's Word is studied, believed and applied. Instead, Catholics and Catechisms today teach that rituals and liturgy are *sacramental,* the necessary means through which God's grace is given.

Origen's view conforms with the teaching of I Peter 2:2 quoted above. Peter instructed newly saved believers that spiritual growth and development results from careful study and feeding on the Word of God and applying it personally rather than from rituals. Peter wrote:

As newborn babes, desire the sincere milk of the word, that ye may grow thereby.

Today, newly born Christians need to grow spiritually by feeding on the Word of God through regular reading and study of the Bible. Feeding on the Word should continue through the life of the Christian. This feeding should take place in church services and also individually as the Christian personally disciplines himself to spend time daily in reading and studying the Word of God.

Origen contended that many in churches, even in his day, started substituting visible signs (liturgy, rituals, statues, etc.) for the spiritual truths they represented. Origen contrasted those needing visible symbols with the spiritually-minded. The more spiritually-minded, he taught, need no more than the spiritual concepts in the Word. Tragically, liturgy and rituals (visible helps which were developed to teach or represent spiritual concepts) became more important for many than the actual spiritual concepts themselves. The problem exists today.

His biographer summarizes Origen's view of sacramental rituals this blunt way:

Visible worship and the sacraments seem necessary for the simple only. Spiritual eating [from the Word] is plainly asserted to be superior to the ritual (pg. 65).

Origen preached a sermon on the passage in John 6:53 where the Lord, using figurative language, said, "*...Except ye eat the flesh of the Son of man, and drink his blood, ye have no life in you.*" In his sermon, Origen pointed out that the Jews and even some of the Lord's disciples had questions about what the Lord said. They asked whether the Lord was actually saying that they should eat His flesh and drink His blood to get eternal life. Origen agreed with their concerns. The Apostle Peter had warned in II Peter 1:20-21 against private interpretation when using or applying scripture without carefully discerning how a passage fits into the clear unified teaching of the Word of God. Therefore, Origen, in his sermon on John 6:53, gave the Biblical basis for a different interpretation. Ten verses later, in John 6:63, the Lord Jesus Himself provides understanding of the passage about eating His flesh and drinking His blood. The Lord explained, saying:

It is the spirit that quickeneth (maketh alive); the flesh profiteth nothing: the words that I speak unto you they are spirit, and they are life.

In this passage, the Lord pointed out that in John 6:53 He had been using figurative language.

Origen in explaining that verse adds a statement which characterizes much of his teaching. Danielou quotes him:

You must realize that what is written in the Bible is sometimes figurative, you must study and interpret it like spiritually-minded men, not like the fleshly-minded. If you take something literally as the fleshly-minded do, it may do you harm instead of nourishing you (pg. 66).

Origen's concerns about taking some things in scripture literally developed from a serious personal experience. Early in his Christian life, he was deeply influenced by Matthew 19:12. In this passage, the Lord Jesus said:

For there are some eunuchs, which were so born from their mother's womb: and there are some eunuchs, which were made eunuchs of men: and there be eunuchs, which have made themselves eunuchs for the kingdom of heaven's sake. He that is able to receive it, let him receive it.

Origen, with a sincere desire to base his life totally on the Word of God, applied the Lord's instructions literally. He had himself castrated. As his spiritual life developed, Origen admitted that he had been wrong in this action. Out of that experience, Origen developed cautions about taking some scriptures literally. He came to see the importance of determining when the Word is figurative and when it is to be applied literally. For example, in Matthew 5:29-30 in the Sermon on the Mount, the Lord uses figurative or teaching language. After warning men about looking on a woman with lust, the Lord Jesus said:

> *And if thy right eye offend thee, pluck it out, and cast it from thee: for it is profitable for thee that one of thy members should perish, and not that thy whole body should be cast into hell.*
>
> *And if thy right hand offend thee, cut it off, and cast it from thee: for it is profitable for thee that one of thy members should perish, and not that thy whole body should be cast into hell.*

Was the Lord in this passage actually teaching that in order to avoid temptation and sin that Christians should pluck out an eye or cut off a hand? No!

It was in this type of context that Danielou quoted Origen as warning:

> *You must realize that what is written in the Bible is sometimes figurative, you must study and interpret it like spiritually-minded men, not like the fleshly-minded. If you take something literally as the fleshly-minded do, it may do you harm instead of nourishing you (pg. 66).*

Similarly, in Matthew 26:26-28 when Jesus was instituting the Lord's Supper the scripture says:

> *And as they were eating, Jesus took bread and blessed it, and brake it, and gave it to the disciples, and said, Take, eat; this is my body, And he took the cup, and gave thanks, and gave it to then, saying Drink ye all of it; For this is my blood of the new testament which is shed for many for the remission of sins.*

Catholics use this passage as the basis for claiming that at Mass when the priest repeats the Lord's words over the wafer of bread and the wine that they are actually transformed into the actual body and blood of the Lord.

That the Lord was speaking figuratively and that His words did not actually change the wine into His actual blood is shown in the next verse. The Lord referred then to what was in the cup, not as His blood, but as "the fruit of the vine." Jesus said:

> ...I will not drink henceforth <u>of this fruit of the vine,</u> until that day when I drink it new with you in my Father's kingdom.

As in this passage, the Lord frequently used *metaphors*. In a metaphor, one thing is compared to another, by describing it figuratively as that very thing. For example, in Luke 13:31-32, when the Lord Jesus referred to King Herod as a "fox," no one understood him to imply that the ruler was a four-legged animal with a bushy tail.

Likewise, today, if someone displays a photograph and says, "This is my wife." the viewer understands that the photo is not actually the wife, but a picture of her. That is an example of using a *metaphor*.

THE LORD'S SUPPER: GOD'S WAY

The only Biblical instructions for communion in a church are in I Corinthians 11:23-34. In Paul's epistle to the Corinthian church, the Apostle wrote that the Lord instituted the Lord's Supper as a memorial. Paul twice quotes the Lord at the Last Supper telling the Apostles...

> ...this do <u>in remembrance of me</u> *(I Corinthians 11:24-25).*

In giving his communion instructions to the Corinthian Church, Paul repeated these words twice. It is significant that when the Lord said "...this do in remembrance of me," He didn't say that communion was a time when He would be with them bodily.

Neither did the Lord say that communion was a time when believers could be nourished by feeding on His body and blood. Instead, the Lord just said, "this do in remembrance of me." The purpose of the communion service is to cause us to examine ourselves and confess sin remembering that His death and the shedding of His Blood was for that sin. He satisfied the demands of God the Father's justice.

RITUALS CAN BECOME A SUBSTITUTE FOR THE WORD OF GOD

Origen taught that over-emphasizing rituals can become more important than the reality they were meant to symbolize. Tragically, rituals can become a substitute for careful reading, studying and applying of the Word of God.

Origen was quoted by Protestant reformers of the 16th Century when they were attempting to restore Christ's Church to the doctrine and practice of the First Century.

The Reformation developed in the 1500s after the invention of the printing press. Gutenberg's invention made widespread distribution of the Bible possible in the language of the people. As people began to have Bibles and could read and study God's Word, questions arose about differences between the Bible and the teaching and traditions of the evolving Catholic Church.

The key teachings of the Reformation included (1) salvation is based on scripture *alone*, (2) salvation is received by grace *alone*, and (3) salvation results from faith in Christ *alone*.

Those key Reformation teachings produced deep division in the Christian world. It continues today.

Rather than rituals, services in true Bible-believing-and-practicing churches emphasize worshipful music and Bible preaching and teaching. Regular communion services build unity in the church as believers remember that the Lord took the sin which separates them from others in the body of Christ.

CHAPTER 14

THE PAPAL SYSTEM

And he [Jesus] gave some [churches], apostles, and some, prophets, and some, evangelists; and some, pastors and teachers; For the perfecting of the saints, for the work of the ministry, for the edifying [building up] of the body of Christ.
— *Ephesians 4:11-12*

MANY CATHOLIC DOCTRINES, RITUAL AND PRACTICES conflict with the Holy Bible. The Roman church looks to papal authority and actions of Church Councils (with papal approval) to legitimatize changes which become Church *traditions*. This has resulted in conflicts with Biblical teachings and doctrine.

The Roman Catholic Church bases its papal system on Matthew 16:13-18. Following discussion with the Apostles over who He was, the Lord asked:

...But whom say ye that I am? And Simon Peter answered and said, Thou art the Christ, the Son of the living God.

And Jesus answered and said unto him, Blessed art thou, Simon Barjona: for flesh and blood hath not revealed it unto thee, but my Father which is in Heaven. And I say also unto thee, That thou art Peter, and upon this rock I will build my church; and the gates of hell shall not prevail against it.

For at least 1600 years, the Catholic Church has taught that Jesus Christ was here saying that He would build His Church on the Apostle Peter.

BUT PETER SAYS AVOID PRIVATE INTERPRETATION

Using an isolated passage of scripture to support a position can be wrong if it ignores the overall teaching of the Bible. Peter himself warned against this error which he termed "private interpretation." In II Peter 1:20-21 Peter wrote:

> Knowing this first, that no prophecy of the scripture is of any private interpretation. For the prophecy came not in old time by the will of man: but holy men of God spake as they were moved by the Holy Ghost.

In these two verses, Peter cautioned against private interpretation in studying and applying the Bible. Private interpretation is using a few isolated scriptures to make a point without carefully discerning how they fit into the clear, unified teaching of God's Word.

In the rest of the Bible there is no support for the Catholic interpretation and teaching that the Lord Jesus would build His Church on the Apostle Peter. Consider the following facts:

STUDY THE GREEK WORDS TO AVOID ERROR

God had the entire Bible written in the world's two most precise languages: Greek and Hebrew. The New Testament was written in Greek. Studying the original Greek text can help avoid errors of private interpretation.

In Matthew 16:18 when the Lord Jesus said, "...thou art Peter" He used "petros," the masculine form of the Greek word translated *Peter*. "Petros," the word the Lord used in addressing Peter, means "little rock" or "little stone." In contrast, the Lord then said, "...and upon this rock (petra) I will build my church." The word "petra"— the feminine Greek form— is the word meaning *a massive rock*. So the Lord Jesus was making a contrast here. He was saying, "...thou art Peter [a little rock]; And upon this [massive] rock, I will build my church."

The Lord Jesus said that *the Church would be built upon the confession that Peter made that He, Jesus Christ, was the Rock.*

That Christ is the *Rock* is borne out in earlier scriptures and teachings of both Peter and Paul. Psalms, for example, has many references to Christ as the Rock, including:

For who is God except the Lord: Who is a rock, save our God. (Psalm 18:32)

Let the words of my mouth and the thought of my heart find favour before you, O Lord, my rock and my redeemer. (Psalm 19:14)

II Samuel 22:2 reads:

The Lord is my rock and my strength, and my saviour.

Isaiah 28:16 has a prophecy Christ's coming. The Apostles refer to the passage a number of times in writing the New Testament. Isaiah 28:16 reads:

Therefore, thus says the Lord God; See I am laying a stone in Zion, a stone that has been tested, a precious cornerstone as a sure foundation; he who puts his faith in it shall not be shaken.

What is this "sure foundation" on which the Church is being built? In I Corinthians 3:11, the Apostle Paul says:

For other foundations can no man lay, but that which has been laid, which is Christ Jesus.

In Ephesians 1:22-2:22, the Apostle Paul tells the Ephesian Christians that they became part of Christ's body— the church— through faith in Jesus Christ. He concluded by saying:

Now therefore ye are no more strangers and foreigners, but fellow citizens with the saints, and of the household of God; and are built upon the foundation of the apostles and prophets; Jesus Christ himself being the chief corner stone.

In I Peter 2:3-8, Peter himself acknowledged that Jesus Christ was the foundation on which the Church was being built. The building blocks are the believers in Christ. Peter wrote:

> *If so be ye have tasted that the Lord is gracious. To whom coming, as unto a living stone, disallowed indeed of men, but chosen of God, and precious, Ye also, as lively stones, are built up a spiritual house, an holy priesthood, to offer up spiritual sacrifices, acceptable to God by Jesus Christ.*

That Christ was the *Rock* on which the Church would be built was also the teaching of the Church Fathers through the earliest centuries. The distinguished Church Father, St. Augustine, in the fourth Century, wrote his definitive Second Treatise on the Trinity. In it Augustine said...

> *...the words, "I will build this church on this rock," refer to the faith of Peter who said, "Thou art the Christ, the son of the living God."*

Augustine, even though he supported the papacy, added this very significant paraphrase of the Lord's words to Peter:

> *On this Rock which thou hast confessed I will build my Church, since Christ was the Rock.*

This was the opinion of Christendom at the time. This can be verified from the writings of Euseneus of Caesarea who lived from 266 to 340 and Cyril of Jerusalem (315-386). St. Hilary, Bishop of Poitiers, in his 2nd work on the Trinity, said, "The Rock [petra] is the blessed and only Rock of faith confessed by the mouth of St. Peter."

WAS PETER THE BISHOP OF ROME?

The Word of God creates other questions as to whether Peter was the first Bishop of Rome or the first Pope as the Roman church teaches. In Galatians 2, the Apostle Paul records that he met with Peter and the other leaders of the church in Jerusalem in the Acts 15 council in A.D. 52. At this time Paul said that there was an agreement by the elders and apostles...

> ...that the gospel of the uncircumcision [to Gentiles] was committed unto me, as the gospel of the circumcision [to Jews] was unto Peter; (For he that wrought effectually in Peter to the apostleship of the circumcision, the same was mighty in me toward the Gentiles:) And when James, Cephas [Peter] and John, who seemed to be pillars, perceived the grace that was given unto me, they gave to me and Barnabas the right hands of fellowship; that we should go unto the heathen [Gentiles], and they unto the circumcision [Jews]. (Galatians 2:7-9)

This decision was made in the Acts 15 council held in Jerusalem. Interestingly, Acts 15 indicates that the Apostle James, and not Peter, was the leader in charge. It was James who announced the decisions.

Paul was to be the apostle to the Gentiles. Peter's responsibility was to reach the Jews. This raises the question whether Peter could have been the Bishop of Rome while carrying out a primary ministry to the Jews. Questioning whether or not the Apostle Peter was ever in Rome or whether he was the first pope in no way downgrades Peter. It was Peter among the Apostles and disciples who first recognized and confessed that Jesus was the Messiah. On the Day of Pentecost Peter preached the sermon through which over 3000 people put their trust in Jesus Christ and were saved and baptized. It was Peter who the Holy Spirit directed to the house of the Roman centurion, Cornelius. Peter preached there and Cornelius and people in the Italian band were saved and baptized (Acts 10). God used Peter to write two important Epistles.

However, internal Biblical evidence questions whether Peter was ever in Rome for any period of time. They include:

> (l) Luke, in recording the journey he and Paul made to Rome in Acts 27:1-28:15, never anticipated the possibility of seeing Peter there. Yet, Catholic teaching holds that Peter went to Rome about A.D. 42 and reigned

there as Pope and Bishop of Rome, except for a journey to Jerusalem for the Council ten years later. Even so, as Paul and Luke traveled to Rome in Acts 27, neither seemed to be looking forward to seeing the one who, according to Catholic tradition, was supposed to be their leader. In fact, neither Luke nor Paul are recorded mentioning Peter's name.

(2) Likewise, in Acts 28:16-31 Luke records in some detail the two years Paul spent in Rome teaching and preaching. However, the Bible record never once mentions any contact he had with Peter!

(3) Similarly, in Paul's Epistle to the Romans, written from Corinth in A.D. 58 or 59, Paul announced his intention to come to Rome to preach and get them better established in the faith. He makes no mention of the fact that Peter had supposedly already been reigning there for 16 or 17 years. In his Epistle to Rome, Paul sent warm greetings and compliments by name to 26 other people then in Rome but never mentions Peter (See Romans Chapter 16:1-15.)

(4) Likewise, while in Rome, Paul wrote seven or eight epistles which are included as books in our Bible. Despite the fact that Peter, according to Catholic tradition and teaching, was reigning as Pope in Rome at the time, Paul never mentions Peter. In fact, in the 14 books of the Bible which Paul authored, he mentions Peter in only two. In Galatians, he tells how Peter erred in following some Jewish customs and how he, Paul, "withstood him... because he was to be blamed (Galatians 2:11)." In I Corinthians 1:12 and 3:22, Paul admonished the Corinthians who tended, as individuals, to say, "I am of Apollos"— "I am of Cephas [Peter]"— or "I am of Paul." Instead, Paul said that they were to know that they were "of Christ."

(5) In all of the letters Paul wrote to churches, he never directed those churches to look to Peter for direction and guidance. Nor did Paul ever indicate that Peter was Christ's vicar [substitute] on earth. Even so; the Catholic Church now teaches that Peter and his successors fulfill that duty.

DOES THE BIBLE EVER USE THE TERM "POPE?"

In Ephesians 4:11-12, the Apostle Paul lists for the Ephesian church (and us) the variety of gifted men the Lord gave to His Churches. The scripture says:

And he gave some [churches], apostles, and some, prophets, and some, evangelists; and some, pastors and teachers; For the perfecting of the saints, for the work of the ministry, for the edifying [building up] of the body of Christ,....:

Significantly, the list does not include a "pope," a "cardinal" or even a "priest" among the men who would be used to direct the edifying (building up) of the on-going church.

THE EVOLVING CHURCH

During the long process of *evolving,* the Catholic Church has experienced periodic turmoil. But that has now changed.

Even the dramatic changes produced by the Vatican II Council in the early 1960s were orderly. The Vatican II "peace" may have resulted from the decision made at the tumultuous Vatican I Council ninety years before. In that 1869-71 Council, Papal infallibility was adopted as a church dogma for the first time. This dogma gave the Pope the absolute power which produced unanimity at Pope John Paul's Vatican II in the early 1960s.

The Vatican I Council (1869-71) was called by Pius IX. Approval of the dogma of papal infallibility soon became its purpose. Approval by the bishops of papal infallibility would have quieted widespread opposition produced by an 1854 personal decision of Pius IX. In that decision, the Pope declared that Mary, the mother of the Lord Jesus, was immaculately conceived without original sin. She would therefore herself be without sin.

Widespread opposition developed within the Church to this Papal decision. The opposition was Bible-based. Bishops who opposed the decision of Pius IX pointed to Mary's *Magnificat* in Luke 1:46-47 where the scripture says:

> And Mary said, My soul doth magnify the Lord. And my spirit hath rejoiced in God my Saviour.

Opposition to the Pope's proclamation argued, "If Mary had indeed been conceived without sin and remained sinless as Pope IX proclaimed, Mary would not have needed a Savior." Those who opposed the Vatican I effort to declare the Pope infallible said that if the Council were to declare popes infallible it would, in effect, approve the personal decision Pius IX had made about the sinlessness of Mary sixteen years earlier. Previously, such major doctrinal decisions had been made at specially called Councils of Bishops and Church leaders.

Much of what unfolded at Vatican I in 1869-71 was recorded in both the classic 1911 edition of the *Encyclopedia Britannica* and the 1913 edition of the *Catholic Encyclopedia*.

Although 1100 bishops were eligible to participate, only 600 finally took part. Just over two-thirds ultimately adopted the resolution approving papal infallibility. Almost one-third of the bishops either voted "No" or abstained. Dozens spoke out against declaring the pope to be infallible. When debate was halted, forty bishops were waiting to speak.

Opposition to the papal infallibility decision resulted, not because of unhappiness with Pius IX. He was a long-serving and very popular Pope. The concerns and the opposition stemmed from the precedent which was being established.

An underlying issue which divided the Council was the imbalance in the representation given Italy which had 270 bishops and cardinals voting. The rest of Europe had just 265. The papal states surrounding the Vatican had 600,000 people represented by about 65 bishops or cardinals. On the other hand, twelve million German Catholics were represented by just 19 bishops.

Bishops who were opposed pointed out that declaring Popes to be infallible would approve the periodic heresies and immoralities of certain popes in the thousand years before Vatican I. When attempts were made to name some of these historical problems, speakers were shouted down.

From the pulpit, speakers cited well documented faults, heresies, contradictions, immoralities and reversals of doctrinal pronouncements made by earlier popes. Finally, one German bishop summed up the dilemma, saying:

> *If you then proclaim the infallibility of the present pope, you must either prove, that which is impossible to prove, that the popes never contradicted each other or else you must declare that the Holy Spirit has revealed to you that the infallibility of the papacy dates only from 1870.*
>
> *Are you bold enough to do this?*

The French Bishop, Felix Dupanloup of Orleans, summed up the case for the opposition, saying...

> *...if we declare Pius IX infallible, we must necessarily, and from natural logic, be obliged to hold that his predecessors were also infallible. Well, venerable brethren, here history raises its voice to assure us that some popes have erred.*

Seeing that the Council was in such turmoil and so deeply divided in favor of infallibility, Archbishop Peter Richard Kenrick of St. Louis refused to deliver his presentation. He left the Council on June 4, 1871 and returned home. He received a tumultuous welcome on his arrival in St. Louis.

Kenrick was one among many opponents. Many bishops and three cardinals refused to announce the infallibility decision in their dioceses. Most eventually submitted to Rome, but continued to hold their personal reservations.

When Papal Infallibility was adopted by the 1869-71 Vatican I Council, future dissension was eliminated. Peace was ensured through the decision because future Popes had been given absolute authority. Giving popes absolute authority has eliminated future disputes.

CHAPTER 15

SOME PEOPLE ARE TRULY SAVED – BUT MANY ARE NOT

> *For God sent not his Son into the world to condemn the world; but that the world through him might be saved. He that believeth on him is not condemned; but he that believeth not is condemned already, because he hath not believed in the name of the only begotten son of God.*
> *— John 3:17-18*

THE TITLE OF THIS CHAPTER is based on the words of the Lord Jesus Christ. In the *Sermon on the Mount*, the Lord said:

> *Enter ye in at the strait gate: for wide is the gate, and broad is the way, that leadeth to destruction, and many there be which go in thereat: Because strait is the gate, and narrow is the way, which leadeth unto life, <u>and few there be that find it.</u> (Matthew 7:13-14)*

Multitudes are in churches but, in Matthew 7:13-14, the Lord says that only a few people will find the way of salvation. The Lord's words are tragic but they are Biblical. Yet, it is not God's desire that any should die and go to Hell separated from God by sin. The Apostle Peter in II Peter 3:9 says that the Lord...

> *...is longsuffering [patient] to us-ward, not willing that any should perish, but that all should come to repentance.*

God's patience is demonstrated in the life of the man Catholics remember as St. Anthony of Padua. His story is told in the book, *SAINT ANTHONY: The Man who Found Himself.*

Published in 1958 by Franciscan Herald Press, the book tells the unusual but thrilling story.

The subtitle, *The Man who Found Himself*, stems from the fact that according to Catholic teaching Anthony is the saint to pray to when lost things need to be found. The fascinating book tells how near the end of his life, Anthony of Padua found that the assurance of salvation he had worked all his life to earn or deserve could only be received by faith as a gift from God.

Born in 1195 A.D. in Lisbon, Portugal, Anthony (named Fernando as a baby) spent most of his life frustrated while doing the good works for which the Church later named him a saint. Anthony spent his life trying to get good enough to go to Heaven. The book shows that:

> *Anthony was restless and unsettled as a teen-ager in a rich and important Portuguese family. He joined an Augustinian monastery seeking to better know and serve God. St. Augustine, patron of the order, had said, "Our hearts were made for Thee: and they are restless till they rest in Thee." That was Anthony's goal.*

After eight years as a scriptural scholar and his ordination as a priest, Anthony was still restless. He left the Augustinians and joined the Franciscans. The followers of St. Francis were being martyred in Morocco trying to win the heathen Muslims to Christianity. Anthony believed that a man who loses his life in God's service will find salvation. So to win salvation through martyrdom, Anthony went to Morocco. His frustration continued and grew when the Muslim caliph quit killing Christians.

In seeking another way to serve...

> *...Anthony headed for Italy to meet with St. Francis. As a Franciscan, Anthony served for a time as a servant, cooking and cleaning for his fellow friars before finding great success as a preacher. Further success came as a theology teacher and an associate of both St. Francis and Cardinal Ugolino who in 1227 became Pope Gregory IX.*

Each advancement brought excitement and success, even though restlessness and frustration always returned. *Something was Missing* in Anthony's life.

At age 36, as he was nearing death, Anthony found what was missing. A long time friend, Ruggiero, who stayed with him until his death related the story. Anthony told him:

I have always thought of myself as trying to follow Christ; trying to unite myself to Him. I have sought Him and I have thought of all my difficulties and trials and struggles, sacrifices and temptations as things to be overcome in order to reach Him. I have thought of this union [with Christ] as a reward to be earned, an ideal to be attained, and I have been restless to attain it. I realize now I have been wrong.

Ruggiero, who traveled with Anthony for years as a Franciscan, said: "Wrong? But, Anthony, what are you saying? Surely that is our life as Christians? We are pilgrims who must press forward to the goal which is union with God....I know He died for us, and has given us His example and His grace, but we can't really be with Him until we die. In the meanwhile we must just do our part."

Anthony replied:

Oh, Ruggiero, you speak in exactly the same way I have thought for so many restless years; that is why they were restless. As I said, I thought of my difficulties as things to be overcome in order to reach our Lord....I thought the possession of my Saviour as a prize to be won — now I realize that it is a gift already bestowed....It is what St. Paul meant when [in Ephesians 3:17] he said, "May Christ find a dwelling place <u>through faith</u> in your hearts. Realizing this has suddenly put everything into perspective.

"It has certainly changed you," observed Ruggiero, gazing into Anthony's face. "I have never seen you look so calm." His friend added, "Your restlessness is over."

Anthony died shortly thereafter in a convent in Padua. Ruggiero said, "If I have my way, for his tomb, I will suggest those words of St. Augustine which he loved so much:

> *Our hearts were made for Thee, and they are restless till they rest in Thee.*"

The good news, as Anthony and multitudes of others have discovered, is that those who see themselves as sinners needing forgiveness and a new life can have it as a gift. They only need, *by faith,* to personally apply what they say they believe about Christ's death being for them and then call on the Lord Jesus. Romans 10:13 promises:

> *For whosoever shall call upon the name of the Lord shall be saved.*

In John 6:37, the Lord Jesus promises:

> *All that the Father giveth me shall come to me; and him that cometh to me I will in no wise cast out.*

To those truly wanting to be saved, God the Father gives the desire for a new life. Jesus said:

> *No man can come to me, except the Father which hath sent me draw him....*

Once we want forgiveness and ask for a new life from Christ, John 1:12 promises...

> *...as many as received him, to them gave he power to become the sons of God, even to them that believe on his name.*

Once we repent and believe, the resurrected Lord and His Holy Spirit come into our hearts. Romans 8:16 says:

> *The Spirit itself beareth witness with our spirit, that we are the children of God...*

That gives us salvation <u>and we can know it</u>. In I John 5:11-13 the Apostle John says:

> *And this is the record, that God hath given to us eternal life, and this life is in his Son. He that hath the Son hath life; and he that hath not the Son of God hath not*

life. These things have I written you that believe on the name of the Son of God; <u>that ye may know that ye have eternal life.</u>

The Lord wants us to <u>*know*</u> we are saved so we can we show others the way. Don't spend your life in restlessness as Anthony did. <u>By faith</u>, receive God's gift <u>now</u>.

Once I knew that I had believed *on* Christ and what He had done for *me,* I had the same reaction Saul of Tarsus had. When Saul met the Lord Jesus on the road to Damascus, he believed on the Lord Jesus Christ. He was saved and became the Apostle Paul. Acts 9:6 records the first words out of Paul's mouth. They were:

Lord, what wilt thou have me to do?

Once I truly believed that what Christ had done on the Cross was for me *personally,* I knew I had to tell others. The Lord tells us to do it and has a wonderful promise for those who do so. In Matthew 10:32 the Lord Jesus said:

Whosoever therefore shall confess me before men, him will I confess also before my Father which is in heaven. But whosoever shall deny me before men, him will I also deny before my Father which is in heaven.

Tell others what you know He has done for you. Tell them of the changes He has made in how you think, how you feel and how you make decisions. Tell how, through knowing Christ took all the punishment for your sin on the Cross, the fear of death is taken away. Hebrews 2:16 says that Christ died in our place and delivered...

...them who through fear of death were all their lifetime subject to bondage.

As the Lord said in Matthew 7:13-14, only a few find salvation. However, some in both Catholic and non-Catholic churches can give a clear-cut testimony that Christ took all of their sins on the Cross. By faith, knowing they were lost and deserving Hell, they have come to Him for forgiveness and *a new life*. In this way, they have been saved and *born again*.

They should know it and be sure about it so they can tell others. However, because of poor (or wrong) teaching in some churches — or a lack of getting grounded in the Bible after salvation — some may be saved and have a changed life but do not have the full assurance God wants all to have. Others who are lost and still in their sin spend their lives trying to earn what can only be received *by faith* as a gift from the Lord.

When I truly believed that what Christ had done on the Cross was for me *personally,* I was born again. I Peter 2:2 then tells the new Christian what to do:

> *As newborn babes, desire the sincere milk of the word, that ye may grow thereby.*

Christians should set a goal of reading through the entire Bible during the first year. Start with the basics — what I Peter 2:2 called "the sincere milk of the word." The Gospel of John is the best place to start. John 20:30-31 concludes John's Gospel saying:

> *And many other signs truly did Jesus in the presence of his disciples, which are not written in this book: But these are written, that ye might believe that Jesus is the Christ, the son of God; and that believing ye might have life through his name.*

The Gospel of John was written so that people could believe and be saved. When reading the Gospel of John, notice how the recurring words like *believe, trust, condemned, eternal life* and *everlasting life* apply to your personal situation. Reading and digesting the Gospel of John is a blessing and will build an assurance of salvation.

Genesis is the Bible's first book and it is the foundation for the rest of God's Word. Make reading Genesis an early goal.

Each day will go much better if it starts with a spiritual breakfast from the Word of God. In Matthew 4:4, the Lord Jesus said:

> *Man shall not live by bread alone, but by every word that proceedeth out of the mouth of God.*

If most of us were to eat only <u>once</u> a day, how strong would we be physically? Developing the practice of getting more than one spiritual meal each day is essential.

Once John and Genesis are read in the morning (several chapters at a time), start reading through the New Testament. Read Acts to see how the early church did things. Then alternate the Gospels with the Epistles. The Apostle Paul said he wrote his Epistle to the Church at Rome so...

> ...that I may impart unto you some spiritual gift, to the end ye may be established (Romans 1:11).

The Holy Spirit had the Apostle Paul write his Epistle to the believers in Rome to give them a better understanding of the salvation they received when they believed. It will do the same for us. Reread it frequently.

Reading at least two chapters a day in the New Testament will enable the believer to read the entire New Testament four times a year. Reading scriptures faithfully brings us face-to-face with things we need to do and be. It can be helpful to reread certain passages of scripture (like the Sermon on the Mount, Romans 5-8, etc. monthly.)

Reading Psalms and Proverbs regularly makes them a very real part of our lives. The Holy Spirit then brings them to mind when they are needed.

When you start daily Bible reading, I recommend (and personally use) the King James Version. I made that decision after initially trying and comparing many others. My basis for recommending the King James is summed up in a twelve page study I published years ago. It is titled *Six Ways Bible Translators Go Wrong*. It is useful in evaluating both existing and the new translations publishers issue almost annually, often backed by massive public relations and advertising campaigns. For a free copy of my *Six Ways Bible Translators Go Wrong*, send a request to me, John Stormer, P.O. Box 32, Florissant, MO 63032.

To any reader who has not yet made the decision to trust Christ fully for salvation, II Corinthians 6:2 says:

Now is the accepted time: behold, now is the day of salvation.

Do you want the new life and the forgiveness that God has for you? Do you believe that Jesus Christ is God, that He died for your personal sins on the Cross, that He was was buried and then rose again from the dead? If so, right now:

Thank the Lord for dying for all of your sins on the Cross. Then ask Him to come into your heart to be your Lord and Savior? When you do, He will forgive your sins and transform your life and future.

St. Anthony, after years of trying to earn or deserve God's salvation, reached the end of himself. At that point, he simply accepted God's salvation as a free gift. Where are you? Have you by faith accepted Him and all He has for you into your heart and life? Salvation is not a feeling — it is a decision to take the Lord at His Word. New feelings result once we believe and start applying the Word to our individual lives.

***

Individuals who have trusted Christ through reading *Something Was Missing* can get help in starting their daily walk with the Lord.
Write to me :
John Stormer, Post Office Box 32, Florissant, Missouri 63032.

Share a word or note of testimony about how you have been saved and I will send you a free copy of *What Christians Believe*. I'll also send a free copy of my study, *Six Ways Bible Translators Go Wrong*.
What Christians Believe was given to me years ago when I believed. I've distributed hundreds to people who have believed. In a series of very short, easy-to-read chapters, the book poses questions new believers often ask. Instead of just giving answers, the book simply provides scripture references where the Bible answers can be found.
What Christians Believe will help you get acquainted with the Bible. If you have believed while reading *Something Was Missing*, tell me in a note and I'll also send you the free copy of *What Christians Believe*.
No one will call on you. Nor will your name be shared or used in any other way. I will try to pray for you. Please pray for me.

CHAPTER 16

THE CHURCH YOU CHOOSE WILL GREATLY SHAPE YOUR LIFE

Let us hold fast the profession of our faith without wavering, (for he is faithful that promised,) And let us consider one another to provoke [stimulate] unto love and to good works, <u>not forsaking the assembling of ourselves together as the manner of some is;</u> but exhorting one another; and so much the more, as ye see the day approaching.
— *Hebrews 10:23-25*

FINDING THE CHURCH God wants you to attend should be the first goal for a new Christian. Deciding to attend regularly and faithfully is the most important single decision in life once a person has been saved by receiving Christ.

What a person becomes as a Christian will be largely determined by the church that he attends. Therefore, the right church is vitally important. Consider how a church shapes lives:

(1.) If the church is doctrinally sound, the new Christian will be taught and will learn sound Bible doctrine.

(2.) If the church emphasizes soul-winning, the new Christian's concern for lost people will grow. The know-how to help them find Christ will be learned through the preaching of a godly pastor and the example of faithful believers.

(3.) If the church teaches holy living, and how to use the Bible to establish godly standards for dress and appearance, amusements, habits, customs, etc. the

new Christian will be trained and challenged to build Biblical standards in his life, home and family.

(4.) If God's power is being manifested through the lives of the pastor and people, the new Christian will be challenged also to seek to have God's Holy Spirit power in his own life.

(5.) If the church administers the ordinances of baptism and the Lord's Supper Biblically and safeguards their meaning, the new Christian will never forget the new life received by trusting Christ and the need to live a holy life in fellowship and communion with the Lord and His people.

(6.) If the church operates a Christian day school or strongly supports home-schooling or a school operated by another Bible-believing church, the church is likely to be concerned about the Christian growth and development of children in the church.

How a church measures up in most of these areas can be quickly determined by observation. How sound the church is doctrinally demands special scrutiny. It is essential that the pastor, the church itself, and any organizations with which it is affiliated hold to the sound doctrines of the Word of God and teach them. This insures that members of the church will...

... henceforth be no more children, tossed to and fro, and carried about with every wind of doctrine, by the sleight of men, and cunning craftiness, whereby they lie in wait to deceive (Ephesians 4:14).

To determine whether a church is sound in doctrine and practice, ask the pastor and/or the leaders of the church (Sunday school teachers, etc.) these questions:

(1.) Are all of the Words in the Bible God's Words? Is the Bible totally and completely true and without any errors or mistakes? (See 11 Timothy 3:16-17.)

(2.) Did God make the world and everything in it (including man) in six actual days — resting on the seventh? (See Genesis 1:1-2:3.)

(3.) Is Jesus Christ God? (See John 1:1,14; 10:30; and 14:7-9.) Was He miraculously conceived by the Holy Spirit and actually born of a virgin? (See Matthew 1:18-25 and Luke 1:26-38.)

(4.) Was it necessary for the Lord Jesus to die on the cross and shed His blood to pay for man's sin and then be raised from the dead on the third day? (See Hebrews 9:22. and Luke 24:36-45)

(5.) Are Heaven and Hell real places with Heaven having streets of gold and Hell being a place of torment with real flames which will burn forever? (See Revelation 20: 10-15 and 21:21.)

(6.) Can a person be saved by faith in Jesus Christ <u>alone</u> (without adding baptism, good works, church membership, etc. to his faith even though we should do these things? (See Ephesians 2:8-9; Titus 3:5; and John 14:6.)

(7.) Once a person has been saved by trusting Jesus Christ is he saved forever even though he may sin and fail sometimes? (See John 6:37 and 10:27-29.)

(8.) Do you believe that the Lord Jesus will come back to earth, put down all wickedness and rule and reign over the earth for 1000 years? (See Revelation 20:1-6.)

(9.) If there is agreement with all of these truths, do all of the denominations, associations, fellowships or conventions the church is affiliated with hold to them, teach them in their schools, etc.? (See Amos 3:3.)

If a church is sound doctrinally, all of these questions will be answered with a strong "Yes." There are a few other questions which should be answered with a definite "No." They include:

> *(1.) Do you believe that a person has to speak in "tongues" to be saved or to show that he is filled with the Holy Spirit? (See I Corinthians 12:4-11, 29-31 and 13:8-10.)*
>
> *(2.) Does your church teach or believe that any book, writings, or teachings other than the Bible are inspired by God and therefore equal to the Bible? (See Revelation 22:18-19.)*
>
> *(3.) Is your church or your denomination (if your church is not completely independent) a part of the liberal, Bible-denying National or World Councils of Churches? (See II Corinthians 6:14-7:1.)*

If a church and its leaders cannot answer "Yes" to the first set of questions and "No" to the second, they have departed in some way from sound Bible doctrine and practice.

A church can be completely sound in doctrine and still fail to be a true, living New Testament body of believers. Several additional tests are needed. In His Word, God says that the function of the church and the leaders whom He puts in the church is...

> *...the perfecting of the saints for the work of the ministry, for the edifying of the body of Christ. (Ephesians 4:12)*

The church is the institution that God established to win the lost to Christ and to teach them to do the work of the ministry.

The "right" church does not just teach doctrine and ways to minister. It also provides fellowship and an atmosphere where church members are encouraged to put into practice what they have been taught. Hebrews 10:23-25 says that once we have been saved:

> *Let us hold fast the profession of our faith without wavering; (for he is faithful that promised;) And let us*

consider one another to provoke unto love and to good works; Not forsaking the assembling of ourselves together as the manner of some is; but exhorting one another: and so much the more, as ye see the day approaching.

In a true New Testament Church, everyone in the body of believers has a dependence upon the others and a responsibility to help others live God's way. That is why the Bible teaches that the way to bring fellow believers to face needs and grow stronger in faith is by...

...speaking the truth in love (Ephesians 4:15).

As contradictory as it may seem, a loving church must also be a warring church. The Bible says:

Ye that love the Lord, hate evil (Psalm 97:10).

A church which truly stands for the Bible must actively oppose evils such as abortion, drugs, alcohol, communism and socialism, immorality, pornography, homosexuality, the occult, etc. However, even as it stands against these evils, the church must be careful to remember that the battle is not against the individuals who are promoting the evil. The war is with Satan and the forces of darkness. Ephesians 6:12 identifies the real enemy, saying...

...we wrestle not against flesh and blood, but against principalities, against powers, against the rulers of the darkness of this world, against spiritual wickedness in high places.

The "right church" will, therefore, hate evil and war against it. At the same time, it will love and try to win individuals involved in the sin and wickedness to the Lord.

Summing up: The right church will be sound in doctrine. It will promote holy living. Its people will be trained and challenged to do the work of the ministry. The members will manifest willingness to minister to one another and be ministered to in areas of weakness. Above all, the church will be controlled and motivated by love. Even as it loves, however, it will be warring against wickedness.

All of these functions will result from continual, consistent preaching of God's Word. The Apostle Paul told Timothy...

Till I come, give attendance to reading, to exhortation, to doctrine (I Timothy 4:13).

In a true New Testament church, the pastor should read the Scriptures, and explain them to the people. This is done through verse-by-verse, chapter-by-chapter, book-by-book Bible teaching. In addition there must also be exhortation. This is strong preaching, in which the congregation is challenged to apply God's Word in their lives. Reading and exhortation is followed by doctrine. Doctrine is Bible teaching which shows how the verse-by-verse teaching and the life applications fit into God's overall scheme of things.

The Apostle Paul came to a town in Greece called Berea. He had just been driven out of a town called Thessalonica. As he preached to the Bereans, the Scriptures tell of their reactions:

These were more noble than those in Thessalonica, in that they received the word with all readiness of mind, and searched the scriptures daily, whether those things were so. Therefore many of them believed.

Be a Berean! Commit yourself to finding a church which meets the test of Biblical standards. Then attend it faithfully. This is vitally important, for you will be what your church is; and what you are, your children will be.

ORDER FORM

Order John Stormer's Book...

SOMETHING WAS MISSING

For Friends
  Relatives
  Neighbors
  Church Members
  Co-Workers
  Catholic Pastors
  Other Pastors

Special Quantity Price
1 Copy: $12.95
5 copies: $30   10 copies: $45
Full Cartons of 50 books $100
100 copies (Two Cartons): $175
1000 or more: $1.50 each

Prices include free shipping in the U.S.
Send Checks or Money Orders To:

LIBERTY BELL PRESS
Post Office Box 32
Florissant, Missouri 63032

Please send _____ copies of *Something Was Missing*

Payment of $_____ is enclosed. Ship my books to:

NAME _____

ORG: (If appropriate)_____

STREET:_____

CITY: _____ ST:_____ ZIP:_____

ORDER FORM

Order John Stormer's Book...

SOMETHING WAS MISSING

For Friends
   Relatives
   Neighbors
   Church Members
   Co-Workers
   Catholic Pastors
   Other Pastors

Special Quantity Price
1 Copy: $12.95
5 copies: $30   10 copies: $45
Full Cartons of 50 books $100
100 copies (Two Cartons): $175
1000 or more: $1.50 each

Prices include free shipping in the U.S.
Send Checks or Money Orders To:

LIBERTY BELL PRESS
Post Office Box 32
Florissant, Missouri 63032

Please send _____ copies of *Something Was Missing*

Payment of $_____ is enclosed. Ship my books to:

NAME _____

ORG: (If appropriate)_____

STREET:_____

CITY: _____ ST:_____ ZIP:_____